My
Roller Coaster Ride
with God

My
Roller Coaster Ride with God

By Sandra Burnes

XULON PRESS

Xulon Press
2301 Lucien Way #415
Maitland, FL 32751
407.339.4217
www.xulonpress.com

Unless otherwise indicated,Scripture quotations taken from the King
James Version (KJV)–*public domain.*

Printed in the United States of America.

ISBN-13: 978-1-6628-0036-8

Dedication

This book is dedicated to my mother and grandmother who were always there for me. We could always share intimate conversations with true, respectful feelings and no worries of what the others would think. I truly miss these two wonderful women whom I had the opportunity to share my life with.

This book of memories shares all my travels that have led to roller coaster adventures in my life. Hopefully, it will encourage and inspire those who have or are experiencing the same ride. Each chapter holds a memory dear to my heart.

Each city, town, and country holds a tale. The memories are more dear to me than the adventures themselves, as my mind drifts and can never quite break free from the experiences of the past and today.

Even though I have walked many rugged paths and climbed many hills, and am still walking and climbing, I have left my footprints on every path and welcomed each new curve in the road.

But the best part of my journeys are not found in places. The best part of my journey is that comfortable little road of memories that leads to home.

When I see home on the horizon, I know all is well and I am once again thankful for all my journeys, including all the good, bad, and indifferent people who have crossed my path along those dusty, earthbound trails.

Contents

Introduction

I'm not well known or a celebrity, but before you begin reading my story, I think it would be a good idea for you to get to know me. I can start off by saying I am totally blessed. I have a great husband and marriage, which has taken a lot of work on both our parts; it hasn't always been peaches and cream. Looking back, we both see how God has molded us into who we are today and has shaped our marriage. Don't worry, we are still a work in progress just like so many others.

I have two great adult children who are experiencing the same lessons as me at their ages. Hopefully, learning the lessons I've learned along the way will bring spiritual growth. I also have two wonderful granddaughters who play a big part in my life and whom I absolutely love so very much. My greatest passion is being a mom and grandma. It has made me who I am today, and nothing brings me greater challenge, joy, contentment, or treasure than these two roles. I also have two dogs that are my family as well.

I live in the Pacific Northwest, and I especially love its beauty and nature. I enjoy the beautiful seasons we have the privilege of experiencing. I truly appreciate spring, fall, and some parts of winter. I absolutely dislike summer, though; summertime and I do not get along.

I enjoy reading when I have quiet moments without interruptions. A real pleasure of mine is reading the King James Bible. The stories are so heartfelt and speak so much truth. They make you want to learn and know more. I can honestly say you do not need to read horoscopes or seek a fortune teller to know about your life. The Bible already provide us all the details. It is, by far, our life compass. One of my favorite verses is Psalm 119:105, "Your word is a lamp to guide my feet and a light for my path."

The Bible is full of so much history and mystery that fascinates me, but what is absolutely amazing about this great history book is that there is a story for each and every one of us with someone who you can relate to. You know how history repeats itself? Well, the Bible is the number one history repeater. Not only is it a great history book, it is a story of the beginning of how we came to be; it tells of what took place, what is taking place, and where it will end.

There is never a dull moment around my world. I am sure, as you read through every chapter, you will discover my life is filled with many adventures of fun, happy times; sad times; and hurt that is so deep. But as I hang on to the Lord, He is, and has been, my tour guide. He has walked me through many valleys and continues to do so.

Now you know a little about me, but you will discover more as you read on. I truly think the best way to know a person is through their living example. I want my life to be well-written and well-read. I pray my story is a compelling story that inspires others or blesses their day. I am like any other lost sheep trying to find her way and wanting to grow more in my walk with God. What I do know for sure is that

God loves me where I am and where I have been, and He will be my tour guide on this journey called life. So fasten your seatbelts, it's going to be a bumpy ride!

Chapter 1

Growing Up in a Small Town

grew up in a small farming town in Livermore, California, where there was little to do, and everyone knew everyone. You can imagine how that worked. You sure couldn't get away with much without someone knowing your every move and it getting back to your parents. Then again, to some it didn't matter if they were caught, because they were the ones who always played dare, would get a scolding, then back to getting into trouble again.

My folks were much respected and were friends with many. I knew if I did mess up, it would get back to them for sure. Things were quite different when I was growing up, not like in today's world. Families were together more and children were more respectful. My sister and I, and just about every other kid we knew, were raised with respect and good morals. Our parents took an active part in our lives growing up. They worked hard and even took on side jobs so we could have awesome vacations every year and newer clothes to start school.

I grew up in a middle-class family, lived in a bedroom community where everyone in our neighborhood was like family. My dad was a laborer who worked for the Lawrence Livermore Lab for thirty years before he retired. The Lawrence Livermore Lab is still in operation today and is one of the largest contracted government facilities in California. Mom worked for the Livermore Unified School District in the kitchens, and made our school lunches taste way better than normal, because everything mom made tasted wonderful! She worked in the school district for many years before retiring.

I was always the shy kid who never spoke up and defended myself. I think that came from my dad because he was the one who did not like confrontation. My dad was very laid back and did not speak up. He was always so worried about what someone else would think or say that he always just walked away or pretended like everything was great. When I look back, that's exactly the kind of child and teenager I was.

On the other hand, my sister Penny was the sassy one, and our mother had a very bold attitude. Mom was a kind and a wonderful mom, but she was very vocal and spoke her mind and stuck up for what was right. I guess that's why we never had any drama in our family back then. I am sure no one wanted confrontation from my mother being the full-blooded German she was with her extreme temper.

Being the oldest, I was the one in trouble the most with my mother, even if I didn't do it. My sister and I are five years apart, and being the baby, she could do no wrong. I recall how my sister did certain things to get me in trouble which happened frequently. I remember how we would fight, and she would go off and slap and pinch herself until she made

2

marks, then running to our mom crying and holding out her arm saying, "See what Sandie did to me?"

One particular day, my mom was on the phone at the dining room table where I was also sitting as well doing homework. We then heard a sound like slapping coming from down the hall. Mom then hung up the phone, and proceeded asking me, " What the heck is your sister doing?" I then explained that we had gotten into a fight earlier, and she was slapping herself to make marks to get me in trouble. Mom then yelled for my sister, as she came running and crying holding out her arm to show the damage I had done to her. Boy! did my sis ever get the taste of the German army from our mother that day! Mom then apologized to me as she stated that she was so sorry she had not handled the matter in a different way in the past as she gave me a hug.

Here's another incident of my sister's trying ways. Our mom had bought Oreo cookies for our lunches. Mom always packed our lunches for school, unless we were going to buy school lunch that day. She always packed dad's lunch for work as well. Mom specifically expressed for us to stay out of the cookies. Well, of course Miss Sassy Pants decided that no matter what mom said, she was going to do the opposite, which was something she did most of the time.

My mom was busy doing laundry, hanging out the clothes. I was out riding my bike when I heard my mom yelling for my sister. I pulled up in the driveway and asked why she was yelling. Mom asked if I had seen Penny anywhere; I told her the house was the last place I had seen her. Mom and I went back in the house calling her, and then went up and down the street yelling for her. Even some of the neighbors joined in. But there was no answer or reply.

We were really worried. My mom was crying and frantic; everyone was distressed. My dad arrived home from work and joined in franticly looking for Penny. At this point, my folks decided to call the police. We came in the house to do so, and just as my dad picked up the phone, we heard this crackling sound coming from down the hallway. We stood there for a moment to pinpoint exactly where the sound was coming from, and we realized it was coming from the bedroom my sister and I shared. The sound was coming from under my sister's bed. As my dad bent down and looked, there was Penny grinning from ear to ear with cookie all over her face, crumbs in her hair, and a mess all over the carpet with a finished bag of Oreo cookies.

That was the first time I had seen my dad angry as he spanked my sister. It was out of anger, but also relief from finding her and seeing she was ok. I remember Mom and Dad expressing that maybe next time Penny would listen. However, those were lessons she never learned by.

Penny and I weren't raised with a silver spoon, but we were raised with love and morals. We were raised like most American families. Sometimes after dinner, my sis and I would do our homework, then all of us would sit down and watch family TV shows or play board games. My sister and I were very blessed and fortunate to have experienced that life.

But through my walk of childhood, I have seen families that were torn. As a child growing up, I always had a big heart for hurting people and wanted to be their friend or rescue the underdog even though I was very shy. I used to get my feelings hurt easily, but I hate it when others are hurting. I don't know why I am that way but perhaps it is the way the Lord works through me.

I also loved animals and have a very big heart for them still today. I would always rescue a stray that would come around the neighborhood or bring one home when I was out on one of my exploring adventures.

I always thought we were a nice Christian family who knew and believed in God and Jesus, especially because we were nice people, helped others, and went to church occasionally. We also watched Christian shows during the Thanksgiving and Christmas season. I remember when we would drive on the weekends to visit relatives who lived in the Bay Area, my dad would start singing "Jesus Loves Me," as we would all join in and sing along. When I look back at those days, I see a close and loving family that had great relationships with not only our immediate family but with other family members and close friends as well.

When traveling to the Bay Area, we would cross the Dumbarton bridge, which was always windy. The wind would kick up, and the tumble weeds appeared like people running dodging the oncoming traffic. My sis and I thought it was rather comical, we would laugh so hard at those running tumbleweeds. My dad would join in and narrate like he was at a football game calling out the players. Our dad was a big sports fan, especially when it came to football. Till this day when I see tumbleweeds blowing across the road, it brings me back to that place at a young age and makes me smile, and sometimes it makes me laugh.

At a young age I was always so fascinated with mystery. I would be the one who would always go explore the old vacant houses and buildings with some of my friends. I was a big Nancy Drew and Hardy Boys fan, always reading their books or watching them on TV. Maybe that is where my mysterious imagination came into play. But all in all, when I lay my head down at night, I think back of a family with lots of great adventures, great times, and great memories, with the love of a family in our little community town of Livermore.

Chapter 2

Remembering
The Sixties

rowing up in the sixties in California was a time of hippies, peace, and love, especially in San Francisco. Haight Ashbury and Market were in its heyday, certainly during the famous Summer of Love. Young dreamers converged in the Haight by the thousands. It was the birthplace of the hippie movement, marked by peaceful protests and psychedelic experimentation.

This was around the year of 1968 when my Aunt Gina, Uncle Bob, my cousins Valarie and Karen, Uncle Josh, Aunt Jane, and their boys came down from Washington for vacation. They wanted to go to the wax museum and visit Fisherman's Warf. It became an experience we all will never forget. The hippies came right up to the car window. I remember Aunt Gina's facial expression as she told my dad we needed to get the heck out of there, she had seen enough.

We had a great time at the wax museum. It was so quiet as there weren't a lot of people that day. We walked around admiring all the figures, which were encased by glass so clear you didn't even know it was there. We were in the scary section and my Uncle Josh was bending over to see what was in a coffin, when all of a sudden, his head hit the glass. It made this awful frightful noise that scared him, us, and other visitors. I will never forget the look on his face. My dad made the comment, "Well Josh, what was in that coffin?" Being the card, my uncle was, he came back with some funny reply because I remember everyone laughing.

Our family from Washington did not come down to California as often as we went up to the Pacific Northwest, but when we did get together, it was nothing but fun and lots of laughs. My dad's family played a big part in our lives when we visited. One year, on one of our many Washington vacations with them, my sister and I were spending the weekend with our cousins, Valarie and Karen, when Aunt Gina ran to the store while our Uncle Bob was helping a neighbor. Aunt Gina had bought gumdrops prior to our visit and had stuck them way up on the top shelf of the cupboard. Us girls decided while everyone was not around, we were going to sneak a few gumdrops.

Now, my aunt always had soapy water in the sink with a little Purex, because she was constantly wiping things down. Valarie climbed up on the counter to reach for the candy. She did not realize that the bag was open, however, there went most of the gumdrops into the soapy sink water. We hurried and grabbed all the gumdrops, rinsed them off fast, laid them out on a towel, and sprinkled sugar on them so they looked like the originals. Then we hurried and put them back in the bag and back in the cupboard, shook the towel out and put it in the hamper, and refilled the sink with fresh soapy water. My aunt never knew what we had done until years later when we told her. She did claim she thought there was something strange with the way those gumdrops tasted. We all laughed about it.

Life was very different back in this time, we had rotary phones and black and white TV. The phones came in multiple colors; ours was green, that beautiful olive green, lol. We also had velvety gold and orange furniture along with olive green carpet that matched our rotary phone.

Color television did not come out until the 70's. I still remember watching all those old-time favorites, like *Lost in Space*, *Dark Shadows* with Barnabas Collins the Vampire, and *Bewitched*. Then there was the *Flip Wilson Show* our family got such a kick out of. Flip was a real funny comedian, and he was known for his famous line, "Try it, you might like it." That became one of our family sayings. Mom used it when she made a new dish for us to try.

Mom, Grandma, and I always took summer walks in the evenings. We felt safe to walk anywhere in our neighborhood, except this one night. We had walked up our street and around the block, and while we were enjoying our walk, we heard a car racing and screeching as it speed around the neighborhood. Out of nowhere, it was coming down the street we were on and started to chase us as we ran. We ran up the closest driveway and squatted down in front of a car. I was crying so hard and remember how scared I was. My mom, on the other hand, was so ticked that she yelled at the top of her lungs. I knew if those people stopped that car, they would have no idea who and what they were up against with my mom and Granny's German temper.

My dad heard Mom's yell as well as everyone else in the neighborhood. The owners of the house ran outside and told us to come in, telling us they had phoned the police. We were only a block away from our house, and as the car squealed around the corner down our block, my dad grabbed a heavy piece of driftwood we had on our front porch and hurled it at the car. Not much longer after that, we heard police sirens. Later, we heard that the reckless driver was finally caught. That defiantly was a summer night we will never forget!

Across the street from us lived an older couple who became very special to us. They both were from Boston, and we just loved their Boston accent. Her name was Pearl and his was Lloyd. Pearl loved to sew and made all kinds of things for our family; she also made dolls and doll clothes. Every week, Mom went over and set Pearl's hair in rollers. One Saturday morning, Pearl asked my mom if she could take her to the fabric store because they were having a big sale. We all piled into the car and laughed at Peal's expressions with her Boston accent the whole way. She was a hoot to shop with.

As we were leaving the fabric store, there was what we thought to be a male mannequin standing by the door wearing a suit. On our way out, Pearl walked over to feel the mannequin's suit material, raving about how nice it felt. It turned out that the mannequin was not a mannequin after all, it was a real person. As Pearl was tugging on the material, the mannequin turned to her and said, "Thank you, I am glad you like it." She jumped back, and my mom, sister, and I laughed so hard. Pearl told the gentleman how sorry she was, but he joined in the laughter and said maybe he should take up a mannequin job. He was actually waiting for his wife who just happened to walk up on all the commotion, asking what was so funny. She thought the story was hilarious, too. I am sure it became the talk of the fabric store and that gentlemen for years to come.

The neighbors to the right of us were also like family. My mom would make extra money cleaning house for them occasionally. Liz was very nice, but staunch and very proper. She always wore a dress with a scarf, her hair always in a bun, and she always wore pearl earrings. Her husband, Pat, always wore a suit and a hat that went along with it. I don't remember what kind of work they did, but by the way they dressed and their mannerism, I believe it was something important. He looked like the actor Humphrey Bogart; and he always smoked a pipe. I still can recall the sweet apple tabaco smell he always used.

I will never forget one morning, my folks had just left for work, and my sis and I were getting ready for school, when we heard sirens which sounded very close. We both ran to the front room window and realized the ambulance was in front of Pat and Liz's. I ran next store and found Liz crying as Pat's lifeless body lay on the floor as the medics were working on him. I will never forget his ash grey face and his eyes rolled back in his head. I ran home and called my mom to let her know what had happened, she in return called my dad. We were all so devastated. My mom kept my sister and I home from school that day. Later that morning, we found out that Pat didn't make it. It was a very sad day for all of us.

Not much longer after Pat's passing, school was out for the summer. My folks planned a trip down to L. A. for a visit with family. Highway 99 was such a long, desolate drive. This trip turned out to be a total nightmare for all of us. I broke out in a rash everywhere and was extremely sick. I started itching and running a fever. My folks took me to the nearest ER. Another medical bill; my poor folks, it seemed they never had a break with me. I had come down with the chicken pox and measles at the same time. We had to cut our trip short. Boy, when the enemy attacked my family, he went way above and beyond.

When I look back at those day's past, I see a freckled faced little girl that was so blessed to have the family I had and all it had to offer. Even if it was full of turmoil and sickness, all my family could ever do, was go with the flow!

Chapter 3

My Adventures in Grade School and Junior High

My elementary school years were, I am sure, like most other's experiences growing up. In grade school all the mothers in our neighborhood took turns in taking us kids to school. As we grew older, we walked. Most of us neighborhood kids went through kindergarten, elementary, junior high, and high school together. Some of us even stayed friends after graduation.

I do remember my kindergarten teacher, Ms. Walker. She was a very tall, lanky woman with shoulder-length red hair. She wore very short skirts and spiked high heels and was very stern. I will never forget her. Like I said before, I was very quiet and shy as a child. Whenever I got into trouble, I would cry at the drop of a hat. Ms. Walker use to make us go stand in the coat closet when we were in trouble for talking. If we were real bad we were sent to the principal's office and would get a swat on the rear or he would hit the ruler on his desk. Boy, if that didn't get your attention.

After recess we always had to line up and walk in formation back to class. This girl in front of me was a real troublemaker. For no reason, she turned around and smacked me on the arm. I then smacked her back. Of course, guess who was in trouble! It was just like at home, always getting into trouble over someone else's story telling. Ms. Walker came right to me, grabbed my arm, and walked me right to the principal's office. I was so mad and upset because the other girl didn't get in trouble at all. The principal asked what happened, and when I explained what had taken place, he accused me of not telling the truth. I was devastated to hear him say that because I was told to always tell the truth and I had.

I then called my mom. When she came to the school and I told her what had happened, she knew I was telling the truth. That day the principal saw the German army in action. I remember her firm voice asking why he had not had the other child come to the office and settle it with both girls. Needless to say, he couldn't answer my mom accordingly.

Everything went well through all the other grades, until I reached the sixth grade. That's when I realized not only kids tell fibs, but adults do as well. I had two classes with difficult teachers at this time. First, I had Mr. Cunningham who was bald and wore black rimmed glasses. He looked like a professor but had the attitude of a grumpy old man. Then, I had Mrs. Havens who was defiantly a grumpy old lady. She reminded me of that teacher in the Cheech and Chong comedy record album. She would yell, "Class, class, SHUT UP!" and then add "thank you" in a calm voice as everyone immediately hushed up and returned to their seats. None of us ever really made waves with these two teachers because they were so mean. We knew the repercussions.

One day, as the presidential election between Nixon and McGovern was completed, Mr. Cunningham was discussing politics with our class. Of course, being in the sixth grade, it was not a real interesting topic to any of us because we didn't understand politics at that age. In the sixth grade, we only focused in on reading, writing, and arithmetic; recess and friends; and waiting for the school bell to ring at the end of the day. That's what was interesting to us, not politics.

As Mr. Cunningham continued, he asked us to raise our hands for which candidate our parents had voted for☐Nixon or McGovern. Of course, some of us raised our hands and some of us didn't. Next, he preceded to tell the students who had raised their hands for Nixon that their parents weren't very bright on voting for him.

Later that evening, when my family sat down for dinner, my folks as usual asked us how our day went at school. As we were eating, I asked my folks who they had voted for as president. They looked surprised and asked why I needed to know. I proceeded to explain that Mr. Cunningham said that parents who voted for Mr. Nixon weren't very bright. Boy, did my folks get really upset. They said it was not none of his business who voted for whom.

My mother decided she was going to take care of Mr. Cunningham that following day. My dad, being the one who doesn't like confrontation, suggested to my mom to let it go and they could approach Mr. Cunningham on the issue during the typical school conferences. Of course, my mom was never the type of person who waited or thought the problem would go away or be forgotten about. No, she took care of things right then. The next day, my mother and her German attitude, took action. She went up to see Mr. Baldy as she called him. I guess she put him in his place. Of course, he denied saying those things, telling my mom I must have misunderstood what he had asked. I really dislike being called a liar, especially when I know I am telling the truth.

Later that evening, my mom asked how Mr. Baldy was towards me the rest of the day. I told her he never spoke to me. My dad, on the other hand, told my mom it wasn't necessary to go up to the school and cause a scene with one of my teachers. My dad was embarrassed because he didn't want to have to confront Mr. Cunningham on any subject when it came time for parent teacher conferences. My mother had not caused a scene, however, She just wanted Mr. Cunningham to know he was very foolish for putting sixth graders on the spot concerning things they do not understand, especially about politics. Furthermore, it was none of his blankety business who voted for whom. (Blankety was one of her choice words when she got upset with someone instead of saying the real word, which she did sometimes use.)

Toward the end of the school year, the most embarrassing, humiliating thing happened to me with both of these teachers. I was absent for a couple of days due to the flu, so when I returned to Mr. Cunningham's class, he told me to go over to Mrs. Havens class. He did not tell me why, he just mentioned for me to go there. When I walked over to Mrs. Haven's class, opened the door, and approached her, she asked me what I was doing there. The class was taking a test and I had interrupted. I proceeded to tell her that Mr. Cunningham had sent me over. She then told me to go back to Mr. Cunningham's class and ask him why I was supposed to be at her class. When I got back to my home room, Mr. Baldy asked me why I was back so soon. I answered that Mrs. Haven's class was taking a test and she said I had interrupted them. Oh my gosh, what came out of his mouth next was unbelievable. He looked at me raised his voice and said, "That's why I sent you over there dummy, to take the test."

Some of the class laughed at his outburst and some just sat there in amazement that he would say something like that. Right then, it felt like a knife was struck through my heart. I closed the door and headed down to the principal's office bawling my head off. I called my mom and she came to the school. The principal, her, and I had a little meeting about Mr. Baldy. I was so terribly hurt with this teacher calling me a dummy right in front of all my classmates. I guess the principal took care of Mr. Cunningham instead of my mom, which probably was a blessing in disguise for all of us.

I was relieved when I left Fifth Street School after six years. I was happy to leave those teachers behind who had caused me so much hurt. But as I walked away, I had this feeling of sadness for the next students who had to deal with them.

I was ready for the new adventures of Jr. High. Now it was time to spread my wings and move on to another dimension in my life. Little did I know the new school year was going to bring some great adventures and some not so good ones. I was starting out at a fresh school with new teachers and new friends but also had the same friends I had spent the last six years with. Oh boy, did we think we were special now that we were in middle school. Being in the seventh and eighth grade was a big step and a turning point. You were supposed to be more grown up stepping away from grade school. Parents expected more from you and so did others around you.

At the beginning of the school year, in each class you were told what was expected of you. Of course, the first rule was not to chew gum in class. Ok, how many students follow those rules when told to do so? Obviously, I was one of them who didn't. One afternoon in my math class, two of us were caught chewing gum; Both of us were made to set an example to the other students. We had to come to the front of the classroom and place our gum on the chalk board at nose level and then stand there with our noses pressed against it. This went on for five minutes, though it seemed much longer. Of course, there came again the embarrassment from the other students laughing. I felt so humiliated as the tears rolled down my face. Why are teachers so persistent on making you feel worse, knowing you are going to be laughed at and made fun of from others? In this case, I could not blame anyone but myself.

PE was a challenge for me. I am not an athletic person at all. The physical education teachers thought everyone was athletic. I absolutely hated running track and it showed. It was not my thing nor either the hurdles. Those were the worst. I defiantly was not the deer they thought I was. I remember running fast to jump the hurdle and, as soon as I prepared to take the leap, I came to a dead stop right as I approached it. I was constantly made fun of by the other PE students, especially those who could hurdle. But I passed the class with a satisfactory. To me, that was a good enough. After all, I was not going to compete in the Olympics.

While track was definitely not one of my strengths, there were some PE activities I did enjoy, like volleyball and exercising to music. To me, that is what PE should be about, doing the things you enjoy and are good at.

I also believe schools should accommodate students who are better with hands-on assignments, not just those who are book learners. I have always been a hands-on learner rather than book smart. I do know when it came to school tests, and I was given it as a hands-on test, I always passed. Paper tests gave me such high anxiety that I never did well on them. Most of the time I failed, which in turn led to higher stress with your teachers and parents. Oh boy, then it was a battle. You were given more homework by your teachers until you got it right, then put on restriction by your folks until your grades came up. It seemed like your efforts weren't good enough no matter how hard you tried.

School dances were some of the enjoyable times in junior high for me. No matter how low you feel, dancing is the best pick me upper. Some parents thought that us kids were still too young for dances. I truly don't know why some parents were in such an uproar about these dances because there were a lot of chaperones watching you. Some of the chaperones would use scare tactics, like a pair of binoculars which made it look like they were scoping us out. We sure couldn't do anything wrong with all binocular eyes on us. When it came to my mom, she never used a scare tactic; she just flat out did the maneuver. She would walk up to a couple in a slow dance, grab their arms, and push them apart. She then would take one arm of the guy and girl and place each one on each other's shoulders, so they would be dancing arm's length. She was always embarrassing me and the other students with her tactics, but the parents loved her being the chaperone because they weren't as bold as my mom.

As I look back through the life and times of junior high, it really was quite the experience. Most of the girls in junior high were just starting to develop their top half. Some of us had rose buds and some petunias. Of course, I fell in the petunia category. I remember going home so upset at the end of the school year before summer break because all my friends wore bras and I was in a training bra. My mom always enlightened me about how I would get there soon enough and to be careful what you wish for. That summer seemed to fly by and all of a sudden, just before school started, I woke up one morning and noticed my petunias had blossomed into hanging baskets. Oh my gosh! I was so devastated. My mom was right, you need to be careful what you wish for because sometimes wishes do come true. I had to suffer through some smart remarks and teasing from the boys; I am sure some girls at that age can relate.

But all in all, my junior high years were an experience that everyone had to go through. We all realized this was just the beginning of what lay ahead. Little did we know that we had a whole lot more on our journey entering high school.

Chapter 4

Bell Bottoms
And Eight Track Tapes

ach step of my life brought our family more chal-
lenges. It was now the culture of TV shows, such as
Soul Train, American Band Stand, as well as big hair,
bell bottoms and eight track tapes. The enemy was always
putting our family to the test. There was always some new
catastrophe.

The devil loves chaos in families, and believe me, he gave
us our share. But I had parents who pressed on, no matter
what was thrown at them. There was never any mention of
praying about things or asking to be put on a prayer chain
through the church we attended occasionally. But I know my
Aunt Glenda and Uncle Al kept us in prayer all the time, so
that could be why our family was able to press through. My
aunt and uncle never forced their Christianity on anyone in
the family because they knew how some of the family felt
when it came to religion.

I talked to God in those private moments spent alone with Him. I truly believe, looking back, even though we were not a Christian family we still had that little bit of Jesus tucked in our soul, because we knew who He was. I think sometimes that is what we need, just knowing of Him and keeping Him locked somewhere deep in our soul until that total spiritual convection of the heart seeks and truly finds Him. My Aunt Glenda had always told me that God has given us a free will, and we can choose whatever we want to do with that will. It's sad, but the human side of us always seems to go along with the devil and his ways. We are so easily persuaded by him.

As my mind wonders, I see this short girl with long dark hair and big brown eyes trying so hard to please everyone and fitting into all that life had to offer. I see a very timid girl who was always getting into trouble for things that someone else did or said. I had very little self-esteem growing up, and quite frankly, I think that had to do with the peer pressures of life and having a very strict German mother.

Most of my mother's side of the family were pretty much the same in their actions. They spoke the language and always had the upper hand. They were very authoritative, so when they spoke, everyone listened. Of course, my dad never said much because like I stated before, he truly did not like confrontation. Honestly, I tried to do things right because the outcome was no bed of roses for sure; the repercussions were more like the rose thorns. Every time my sister ended up hurt, I was the one who would get into trouble because I should have been paying closer attention to her. I am sure some of you can relate when it comes to younger siblings.

One particular time, my mom dropped my sister and I off at the junior high school to watch a volleyball game. Mom promised to pick us up when the game was over. As we were sitting there enjoying the game, my sister stood up on the bleachers, jumping up and down to cheer our team on. She lost her footing, fell off the edge, and landed on her wrist, which busted all to heck. She was screaming and one of the coaches ran over as I ran to the office to call my mom. As I was explaining what had happened, you could hear the rage in her voice as she said she was on her way. When she got to the school and ran into the gym, everyone was all crowded around my sis trying to comfort her.

We loaded Penny into the car and drove to the ER. The whole way there my mother was mad at me for not having my sister stand on the floor and that I should have told her to do so. Now, do you think for one minute my sister would have listened to me? I think not. Her reply would have been like all other siblings; "You're not my mother so I don't have to listen to you." I can understand my mother being upset because there was never an end from doctor bills, which were especially expensive since my folks did not have good insurance coverage at the time. That explained why they were always making payments. While at the ER, they put my sister in a cast and gave her some pain meds before sending us home.

When we arrived home, the first thing I did was go to my room and listen to my favorite radio station with DJ host Casey Kasem. Music has always been my tranquility to get away from the pressures going on around me. I would get lost into the '60s and '70s music.

Another memory with getting lost into music. It was Labor Day weekend when my folks and some of our relations from southern Cali went to Death Valley to meet up with some other family and friends. While on our way there, us kids gathered in the back of our camper with the coolest eight track tape player my dad had installed. Candace and I would crank up our favorite songs. We always had such fun traveling and listing to our eight tracks.

A couple of days into our camping trip, Molly, one of the girls in our group, and I decided to go for a short ride on our moms' Honda 90 motorcycles. We went cruising on the sandy trails when all of a sudden, she turned in front of me. The next thing I remember, I was flying over the handlebars through the air like Evil Kinevil and landed on my knee. The hot sand felt like I was lying on hot coals. I couldn't get up. Molly said she would be right back as she raced back to camp to get my folks.

As I was lying there in total pain and looking up at the sky, I could hear in the distance a very distinctive "beep beep, beep beep." It sounded like the Road Runner from the Warner Bros.' cartoons. I knew it was Molly reassuring me. It seemed like every couple of seconds I heard that "beep beep." It grew faint after a while, then I didn't hear it anymore. I started to talk to God to please help me and to please send someone fast. Then, out of nowhere, I heard these motorcycle bikes heading my way. I could not see where they were or how far they were from me. Next thing I knew, these two bikers showed up. At that moment, God sent me not one, but two angels. They helped me to my feet and took me back to camp. By that time, my left knee had swollen to the size of a grapefruit. My folks thanked them for bringing me, and my dad and uncle Harold left to get the injured Honda I had wrecked.

My mom and Aunt Charlotte helped me into the camper where they elevated my leg and put ice on it. The swelling in my knee never went down and the pain was unbearable. I was wearing one of my favorite bell bottom jeans at the time, which was the current style. I remember my mom having to cut them off because my knee was so swollen.

We had to cut our trip short to head back home and to the ER. Before the staff could take an x-ray, they had to drain my knee of the fluid so they could get a better picture and to relieve the pressure. As they were prepping me to drain the fluid, I remember my mom getting so upset and my dad leaving the room when he saw the 20 mil syringe with an 18 gauge needle. It looked to me like the size of a miniature jack hammer. The nurse gave me a shot to relax me before the ER doctor proceeded with the torture of draining my knee.

As he stuck the needle into my knee and pulled back on the syringe, I remember all this greenish, yellowish fluid filling the syringe as I watched in horror. I looked over at my mom and she was as white as the sheet draped over me. I started to feel sick to my stomach and I suddenly could not hold back any longer. As I heaved all over the sheet and the doctor as he quickly pulled the syringe out of my knee. The nurse quickly grabbed a small waste basket that was by the bed, and my mom began yelling at the doctor. about inflicting so much pain on me and they should have given me something stronger.

The doctor left the room to change his gown and clean up. Then the nurse proceeded to get fresh bedding and my mom gathered a washcloth from her to clean my face. Next, the nurse administered a stronger pain medication into my IV before the doctor came back to finish the job. What an ordeal to have to go through. After all the fluid was drained from my knee, I was wheeled down to x-ray. The x-ray had shown that I had torn ligaments and a torn cartilage

I then was set up to see a specialist that week. My folks and I met Dr. Chan, this little short Asian doctor who was very kind and soft spoken. He proceeded to explain the status of my knee and how he was going to have to go in and repair the damage. That week I was scheduled for surgery.

Afterwards, I was put in a cast and had to walk around on crutches. I remember Dr. Chan telling me that as soon as my knee started healing, it was going to really itch. He informed my folks and me to not stick anything down inside the cast because it could catch on the stitches and tear them open, resulting in more problems to deal with.

After about a week, my leg was itching so bad because it was healing and being in the cast was very hot and sweaty. Right then, I did the unthinkable. On my own, I took a wire coat hanger, untwisted it, and stuck it down into the cast to slightly scratch where it itched. Well, guess what? I tried pulling the hanger back out and it would not move; it was caught on something. I attempted for the longest time to loosen the hanger from whatever it was caught on. I truly was afraid to call out to my folks. I was scared to death to approach them with this wire hanger sticking out of my cast, but I knew I had to sooner or later, so I might as well take the chance. I thought I might end up in the hospital with a coma once my mother saw what I had just done

I mustard up all my strength. My heart was beating so loud, I thought my folks could hear it as I hobbled out on my crutches. When I approached the dining room where they were sitting at the table having a discussion, I remember the look on their faces as I said in a shaky voice while tears were rolling down my face. "I'm sorry, please don't get upset." Well I should have known that wasn't a very bright thing to say as my mom went psycho on me. You can only imagine what happened next. I thought my mom was going to rip the cast off right along with my head and my dad was going to join her. My sister was laughing like she usually did. I kept yelling how sorry I was and how I knew it was so stupid of me. My mom was so mad that she was shaking. My dad immediately noticed my mom turning beat red as he told us to hurry and get in the car as they were going to take me to Dr. Chans office.

All I could think about on the way there was how I had added an extra problem to my already not-so-good situation. I was crying and thinking, "Ooh my gosh, they are going to amputate my leg for sure now." Just about the same time I was thinking that, those exact words came out of my mother's mouth as she whipped her head around and looked at me with that look moms always give when they are ticked off. Her German blood was boiling. I knew then I was in the deepest of deep trouble.

My dad focused on keeping us and himself calm. In his soft tone he said, like he always did, "Just calm down, Bonnie and Sandie. Let's wait and see what the doctor says." Mom at this time was shouting at my sister to quit her laughing, she wanted to know what was so funny. Penny was quiet for a short time but then went back to laughing until my mom mentioned when we got to the doctor's office she was going to have the doc amputate her tongue along with my leg. Oh my gosh, then we both started bawling and caring on!

When we arrived at Dr. Chan's office with me hobbling in with this metal sticking out from my cast, the nurse took us right to a room. When Dr. Chan saw the damage that he specifically ordered me not to do, he instantly turned into a Chinese warrior which scared me tremendously. He then had me sit on the bed so he could cut the cast off. As we all watched, expecting the worst, his face went from Chinese warrior to the sweet Dr. Chan I had first met. I knew then everything was ok, no damage done. I started crying because I was so relieved. Dr. Chan wrapped my leg in a soft cast which was some kind of cotton and Ace bandage. He told me to just rub and pat when I itched. He also told me in a firm, Oriental voice that he better not see me in his office again until it was time to remove the cast completely. I reassured him I would not do it again. My mother then replied, "you better believe she won't do it again, because I personally will remove the cast myself." Knowing my mom, that's exactly what she would do.

On our way home, my mom remarked how lucky I was to not have ripped my stitches open. I was thanking God for sending me a guardian angel to protect me from the doctor and my angry mother. But I think the blessing from all this was it saved my folks from having to add to their mountain of doctor bills. So, there was some good that came out of this frightful experience.

After three to four weeks of my knee healing, I was back to my normal self. I had an ugly scar that made my left inside knee look like a railroad track from where the staples had been. And to me, being who I was at that time, it seemed like my whole world was coming to an end because of that scar. I know better as an adult now. I have frequently seen others with something so much worse than me, So with that being said, I am thankful and grateful that all my battles so far have always been fixable. Maybe did not get to wear those dresses above the knee like before, but guess what? I still get to wear my awesome bell bottoms.

Chapter 5

Our Special Christmas Gift and Music Lessons

It was now growing closer to Christmas. My knee was doing well, and my folks decided to stay home. I'm sure that was because the last couple of years had been a financial hardship on them. They didn't want to risk another catastrophe. Not that it couldn't have happened at home. There were catastrophes that did take place at home from time to time.

We had a very quiet Christmas with just friends and family stopping by. Like I said in the beginning of my story, I did not grow up with a silver spoon, but I felt like I did, especially because of all the things we did as a family. My folks did the best they could with what they had. There was so many others I knew who did not experience the same family relations as us or had a mom and dad that were together.

I can see now that my folks always put the family first in everything. My folks always compromised and talked things out. I really think that is what made our family strong.

Everything seemed to work out. Every year when it was my sister's and my birthday, we would go to this Chinese food restaurant in Stockton called, On Lock Sam's. It was our family favorite and our birthday tradition. My folks saved up all year so we could eat there. It wasn't expensive, but finances and budgeting, was the same back then like it is today. And with the mountain of medical bills my folks had all the time, yes, it took them a whole year to save for our birthday dinner. On Lock Sam's had private rooms, each with a drape, where you could eat alone without others watching. Some good friends of my folks, who were my sister's godparents, always came and celebrated with us. I will never forget them. Bill worked at the Lawrence Livermore Lab with my dad so that's how they came to know each other and how we became family friends. Bill and his wife Nancy really played a big role in our lives. They did not have any children, so they did extra things for us girls.

One Christmas, my sister's godparents came by with an extraordinary gift. They delivered a box with a bow on top and these holes on all sides of the box along with what sounded like a puppy inside. We knew then that it was. As soon as we opened it, oh my gosh, inside was the sweetest Dachshund puppy and her name was Little Bit. She was so adorable! Her name fit her perfectly, because she was little and a bit mischievous.

Later my Grandma and her husband came by and we had our traditional German food, such as potato patchinlla, which is one of our family recipes passed down from our great grandparents on my mom's side. There was a wonderful salad and all the other fixings that Grandma always put together. Of course, I cannot forget all the baked goods. There was potato candy, pies, molasses cookies, Pfeffernüsse cookies, and so much more. Food was a big part of all our family get-togethers.

My Grandma had a restaurant in Escalon, California that we visited a couple of times a month on the weekends. We often stayed with her and got so many treats, not only from Grandma's kitchen at home but from her restaurant kitchen as well. My grandmother was an awesome cook, but all of my mom's family were, and still are fantastic cooks.

Our relatives from LA, who we went on vacations with, surprised us all when they drove up in front of our house. We were all surprised to see them.

I began the new year with a new interest in playing the piano. My folks enrolled me in piano lessons. I will never forget my piano teacher. She was a very strict instructor. She had short, gray, bobbed hair and wore wire frame glasses. She had an authoritative voice that had a roll when she said my name. She never called me Sandra. It was Sondra in a very firm voice. She also had a little poodle I took a real liking too. I would pay more attention to the dog then Mrs. Randall sometimes.

I was doing quite well on the piano until I had my first recital. I remember practicing "The Skater's Waltz" hours a day and I played it so well when on my own. Then, when the recital came and I had to get up and play it in front of others, my mind drew a complete blank. I remember Mrs. Randall calling to me, "Sondra, sit straight, look forward, and listen to the ticking of the metronome." I began and the piece started out well, then, all of a sudden, I went blank again. This happened a few times. I just cried as all the other parents and students still clapped for me as I went to sit down. I know the clapping was to make me feel better, but of course I felt horrible since I knew the piano piece and could play it well.

That night there were only two of us who did not do so well with our piano playing. When all was said and done, Mrs. Randall gave me a hug. She told me and my parents that those things happened and that maybe next time I would do better. That was the first time I ever saw a softer side of Mrs. Randall. I guess sometimes hard people have soft hearts. I took piano lessons for about a year, then went on to accordion and then steel guitar. Guess who my teacher was? You guessed it, Mrs. Randall. I was pretty good with instruments, except for recitals.

I was always into music. I loved to sing and dance. That's hard to believe since I was so shy. But it seems like music brings out a bolder side of me. I was always in chorus growing up and in dance. My folks kept my sister and me active in things we enjoyed doing. During the Christmas season, I loved to play Christmas carols on the piano. Sometimes we would all sit around and sing Christmas songs, especially when my Grandma, Aunt Glenda, and Uncle Al would stop by.

We never had any family drama between any of our family members, at least I never knew of any. As we all gathered around and sang "Joy to the World" and "We Wish You a Merry Christmas and a Happy New Year," I felt an overwhelming sensation come over me on how I loved my family and how we survived another year. As the end of the year drew near, I wondered what the New Year would bring me and my family. I knew whatever it brought, we would survive as we usually did because I knew we have an awesome God who is always with us, along with those family members who keep us in prayer.

Chapter 6

Lost in the Woods and Our Camping Bear

ur vacation trips and all our wonderful family adventures stand out in my memories. My family had such awesome camping trips in many great states with all the beauty our Creator created for us.

Another summer saw us heading to Colorado for another family camping trip. I was about eleven or twelve. The campground we arrived at was nestled right in the center of the forest. We were surrounded by huge trees Things were going well the first couple of days until Candace, my sister and I, decided to go exploring on this trail close to our camp. We told our folks we were not going to go far, that we just wanted to adventure a little way up the trail. They told us not to go too far, we'll soon be eating dinner.

So, the three of us girls headed up the path while doing the Hansel and Gretel thing of leaving breadcrumbs to find our way back. Ha! I guess we forgot the part of the story where the bread crumbs get eaten by the birds. And the forest is full of birds, squirrels, and other small creatures that have no idea you need those crumbs for a reason. Of course, the trail broke off into two separate paths. We thought, "No problem, we can go just a little more, then turn around and follow the trail of bread crumbs right back to camp." It didn't seem we walked very far. Then Candace suggested we better head back since it was just starting to turn dusk, so our moms wouldn't be mad at us for being late for dinner. Off we head back down the trail, but we didn't see many bread crumbs, we walked and walked and walked for a very long time but never reached camp.

Somehow, we ended up turned around and were heading further into the woods instead of going the direction we should have been going. We yelled loudly, hoping our parents would hear us. It was getting dark, and we were scared and crying. We then heard motorcycles not far from us, so we started running and yelling in the direction of the sound. We were down in a gully by this hill, and we could see bikers above us. We ran up the side of the hill, by the time we reached the road, the bikers were gone. Then we heard traffic in the distance, so we headed down the road toward that sound.

We could see some head lights, so we knew we were close to people and maybe our campground. We kept walking and walking; it seemed forever. We were starting to get tired, hungry, and cold. Candace and I were saying how our moms were going to be so mad at us. We were almost to the end of the road and we saw two motorcycles not too far in the distance. We started running towards them; about a quarter of the way, we noticed it was our dads.

Now let me mention again both my uncle and my father were laid back men who hardly ever raised their voices. I really don't ever remember my dad or my Uncle Harold extremely mad, except the time my dad found my sister hiding under the bed with a whole bag of Oreo cookies eaten. They both came to a stop as we were crying, so happy to see them. I remember Candace, Penny, and I asking if we could have a ride back to camp. I will never forget what my uncle said in a very stern voice; it really tore our hearts out. He replied, "You three have walked this far, so you can walk the rest of the way" Oh my gosh, we knew we were in hellacious trouble then.

All three of us looked at each other and said maybe we should just stay lost. Then my dad told us we were not that far from camp and if we stayed on the road, we would see the campground. As we headed down the road, my dad told us they were going back to camp to let all the other volunteers and the park ranger know that we'd been found. We walked into the campground crying, though I don't know if it was a happy cry or a cry of knowing we were in big time trouble. It probably was a combination of both.

I remember telling Candace and Penny, we at least get to have one last meal before we died by the hands of our mothers. They both looked at me like I was crazy, then we all started laughing. Of course, we got dirty looks from everyone when we did, we instantly shut up in a hurry. We were so thankful to be back with our families, even if we were in big trouble.

I don't think any of us will ever go hiking again. When us girls thought about it, that walk could have led to an outcome of so many other things. We must have had a guardian angel with us that whole time. The remainder of our years traveling and going camping, we never did another hike without having our folks or a tour guide with us.

Our next camping adventure was our trip to Yellowstone. What a beautiful adventure with all the geysers spewing water from the ground. And there were bears walking around the road while you were safe in your car. You weren't to feed them or put your hand out of the window to pet them, but I wanted too! I remember those bears coming up to our truck window, peering in. I kept asking my folks if I could crawl back into the camper and grab something for the bears to eat. My folks would say, "Sandra Lynn, you were told no! One swipe of those bears' paws will take your arm completely off." As we drove slowly down the road to our campground, the bears just disappeared in the distance.

When we pulled into the campground, the park ranger came around and chatted with everyone. He reminded us not to feed the bears or leave any food out at night. There never were bear attacks or anything; the bears only came around looking for food, which I didn't see anything wrong with at the time. When something's hungry, feed it, right?

As the park ranger was telling us all about the bears and what not to do, my folks kept looking over at me, like, "Did you hear what was said?" I just grinned and thought to myself, "Oh they can think what they want, but I will sneak some food for those hungry, sweet bears. They are just black bears; they don't hurt anyone. And food makes everyone happy! Including bears." After the ranger's speech and my parents' special warning looks at me, we all went sightseeing, I had hoped to get the opportunity to at least pet or feed one bear. Of course, there was so much to see and do, that after a while, I wasn't thinking about an opportunity with a bear.

The next night I asked my folks if I could sleep in the cab of the truck which they agreed, as long as I didn't get up in the middle of the night to feed the bears. "Now, how could they have known that?" I thought. That night when Candace, Joe, Penny, and I finished roasting marshmallows and Uncle Harold drank his last beer, we all parted ways. Our dads closed up the ice chests and put them under the trucks, and our moms made sure all food was put away. We all said our goodnights as I nestled in the cab of the truck. As the lights went out, I just laid there in the quietness looking out the front windshield staring up at the heavens, looking at the stars, and trying to figure out God, His universe, and what lies beyond.

I finally fell sound asleep. Later, I heard my mom quietly calling my name trying to wake me up, I turned toward her, she told me to be really quiet and come in the camper. I asked her why, but she only told me again to be quiet. As I crawled into the camper and noticed my sis and dad sitting on the bed, looking out the window. Of course, I joined in to see what they were looking at. It was a group of bears! As we all watched in amazement, we saw one bear pull the ice chest out from under the truck and open it. With one swipe of his paw, he opened the carton of milk, then sat back and chugged. Next, he dug through the ice and took out what food was there. He didn't hesitate to eat all the Oreos. I was so excited to sit there and watch this bear enjoying himself.

My dad looked out the back window to see if Aunt Charlotte and Uncle Harold were also watching, and sure enough, they were. I remember my dad saying, "Boy, Uncle Harold will be fighting mad if that bear drank all his beer." Of course, my dad was not a happy camper with the bear eating all his Oreos. Mom made the comment, "You have to admit, Jake, this is pretty wild sitting here watching these bears, and we can always get more cookies." After the couple of bears left, my dad and Uncle Harold headed out to pick up the trash the bears left behind.

In the morning we noticed the bears had not only eaten our food from our ice chest, but they had gone food tasting with all the other campers in the campground. And yes, one of the bears did have his own little drinking party with a couple of Uncle Harold's Coors. Uncle Harold wasn't very happy, but I'm sure the bear was. Either it had a hangover, or it will never get into another ice chest again.

The next day, we had one last sightseeing tour of Yellowstone before we had to pack up and end our vacation. That evening, we sat around the campfire and went over the day's sites with my folks discussing where their journey was going to take them next trip. The next morning, we all ate breakfast at the campground, cleaned up our space, and said goodbye to all the other campers we had met during our stay. As we pulled out of the campground slowly and drove past Old Faithful spewing high above the ground, the bears followed us along the roadside. It made me wonder if any of those bears were the ones who had a cookies and milk party or the one wasted from Uncle Harold's Colorado Kool-Aid.

Chapter 7

Family Visits to
the Pacific Northwest

ummers spent vacationing in different states were a lot of fun and made so many happy memories. But, when we traveled up north to visit our grandparents, aunts, uncles, and cousins on both our dad's and mom's side of the family, there was also loads of fun to be had. Of course, there often was some kind of turmoil to go along with it.

My parents usually stayed with my dad's folks, and my sister and I usually stayed with our cousins Valarie and Karen. This one particular year, our cousins had moved into another home, not far from the house we had our gumdrop mishap. Their new home was on a hill and the road was on a downhill slope so when we visited during winter all the cousins got together and went sledding down the hill. What a blast we had!

Winters spent in the Pacific Northwest were awesome because we never had snow where we lived in California.

We were building snowmen out of sand at the beach while everyone else who lived in snow states were making real snowmen. But I will have to say, one year in the '70s, we did get snow. That was the first time Livermore had snow in about 100 years or longer. I remember my dad, sister, and I making snow angels, building snowmen, and throwing snowballs. The snow lasted for quite a few days before the Californian weather turned a little warmer and the snow melted making everything wet and slushy.

I remember our snowman slowly disfiguring each day. Each morning, we looked outside to see what level our snowman had progressed, until one morning we looked out the window and all that was left was the carrot nose pointing upward and the stick arms lying lifeless with no snow body attached. The knit scarf and hat were laying on the wet ground like someone had left them there. It was sad for us because we had had so much fun while it lasted. To us, having all that white stuff made you feel so refreshed and that's all anyone would talk about. Everyone in our community had a story about their snow experience. What conversations we shared.

My mom did most of the cooking when we visited our family. Everyone loved Mom's cooking. My grandma and Aunt Gina, were in charge of the desserts. Those two women could make some wonderful baked pies and cobblers! My favorite was Aunt Gina's blueberry cobbler. Sometimes Val, Karen, my sister, and I would get up early in the morning and heat up some cobbler with a scoop of vanilla ice cream on top. That was our breakfast for the morning. Then we hurried and cleaned everything before Aunt Gina and Uncle Bob woke up. Of course, when Aunt Gina made her way into the kitchen and asked us what we wanted for breakfast, we always let her know we already had eaten. When she asked what we had, before we could answer, she would always finish it with, I am sure that cobbler was pretty good. Oh my gosh, how in the world do adults know what you do, without even being there. I am sure we will figure it out when we become an adult.

My grandma was on the feisty side. She had this crook in her right index finger, so when she would point it at you, you knew she meant business. One night, my sister and I stayed the evening at our grandparents. We were sleeping in the living room while my folks were sleeping out in the camper. We were suddenly awakened in the middle of the night by an extremely loud bang that sounded like a cannon had gone off. We jumped up and ran down the hall to where my grandma was, but she yelled for us to stay back. She had the back door open, with her shotgun going off.

My dad and mom stayed in the camper looking out the window until they knew the coast was clear to come into the house. It turned out a couple of older teens had come up on my grandparent's front porch to steal her lounge chairs. Being the light sleeper Grandma was, she had heard them. She then threw open the back door and let that shotgun rip. The thieves dropped the chairs and took off running toward the driveway where there was a huge pile of bark that had been delivered earlier in the day. Each time her shotgun went off, the crooks ran in circles, I guess trying to focus on where they were going. They tried to run up and over the mound of bark, but each time my grandmother shot under their feet causing them to sink into the bark.

What really made my grandmother so mad was not only them stealing her lounge chairs, but when they dropped the chairs and started running, her first shot ended up blowing off the top of her wishing well my folks had just bought. So that's why she started firing underneath their feet when they were trying to get away.

My dad came in the house and told my grandmother she could not let loose like that in a neighborhood. Her reply was, "Well, I bet they will never set foot around here again." Dad's reply to her was, "Well, heck yeah, I know I wouldn't." Luckily, the police weren't called by a neighbor. This may have been because they knew if anything were to ever go down in the neighborhood and they needed protection, Grandma and her shotgun would be the first on the scene. By the incident that had taken place, we knew we were safe at grandma and grandpa's place, and everyone in the neighborhood knew they were safe as well. Everyone talked about the old American Indian lady with the shotgun and how she was the neighborhood security.

I want to share another story about our times spent at our cousins. The newer housing development that Val and Karen lived, had a lot of sage brush around. (Yakima has a lot of sage brush and orchards. It's the capital of apples, hops, and wineries.) So, what do you get with sage brush and dessert land? Snakes, and lots of them!

One day, my aunt and uncle had run to town and us girls stayed behind. We were going downstairs to the family room, as we approached, we saw this huge snake laying in the middle of the floor. We slammed the door shut, ran upstairs in a hurry, and called my grandpa to let them know there was a humongous snake in the family room and no one was home to help.

About half an hour went by and here comes my grandpa and cousin Jeremy with shovels and burlap potato sacks wearing thigh-high rubber wading boots. We crept down the stairs behind them, as gramps and Jeremy opened the door slowly with shovels raised, as if the snake was going to strike at them. Jeremy suddenly let out this yell and all of us jumped back and screamed. We knew we were doomed! Then my grandpa started laughing along with Jeremy, and both said, "Oh my gosh, it is just a garden snake and they don't eat much." Gramps scooped the snake up with the shovel as Jeremy opened the potato sack and threw it in.

Just as they were leaving, Aunt Gina and Uncle Bob pulled up. When they saw all the gear, they were curious to know what the heck had taken place while they were gone. We told them our story about the huge snake in the family room and how Gramps and Jeremy rescued us. Of course, we over exaggerated some on the size. Gramps related his story about the ordeal and made it a real big one with excitement. Aunt Gina and Uncle Bob were wide-eyed with amazed expressions, they were so entranced listening to Gramps finishing touches. As the snake was still in the burlap bag, Jeremy held it out for them to see. Aunt Gina laughingly told our rescuers that if they had blooded up her carpet with snake guts, they had better change into their cleaning gear because they were going to be put on cleaning duty. Of course, Gramps told her with a smile that she better be thankful that he and Jeremy had just saved all of us from the most venomous twenty-foot snake ever on that hill.

There was never a dull moment around our family, for sure. Our Northwest family always kept you guessing with their stories. That's what made everything so exciting with our dad's family. But whatever the outcome on our travels to Washington, whether it be cruising the Ave, sledding in the snow, granny skits, or snakes in the basement, there was always the closeness and love of a family making memories to last a lifetime.

Chapter 8

More of My
Awesome Travels

s I said before, traveling was always adventurous. Our travels to Utah are also ones I will never forget. Crossing the salt flats into Salt Lake City; they seemed to go for miles and miles, looking like blankets of snow.

The first thing you see when you arrive in Salt Lake City is the Mormon Temple. It's so majestic; it looks like something out of the Emerald City of *The Wizard of Oz*. We couldn't go inside, but they had a visitor center where you could get information on the history of the Temple and Utah. Of course, Candace and I were more excited to be in the home state of the Osmonds, as they were our favorite male singing group. We thought we were extra special to be in their home state. We really hoped we would run into them somehow. We had every album of theirs at that time and had watched every TV special and movie they were in. Of course, we had all the *Sixteen* and *Star Magazines* with all their pictures. (I still have

45

some of those magazines from the '70s packed away today) After our visit to the Mormon Temple, we toured the city.

Our next stop was camping in Bryce Canyon for a couple of days before we headed to Wyoming. We set up camp and took the tour through this beautiful canyon. From what I remember walking through it, the rock formation and colors reminded me of the Grand Canyon in Arizona. There were a lot of similarities. After our stay at Bryce, we headed into Wyoming to Aunt Charlotte's mom and stepdad's place where we stayed for the remainder of our vacation.

I remember they lived way back on some acreage surrounded by mountains. Aunt Charlotte's mom, Bernice, and Bernice's husband, Herman, had a house full of Indian arrow heads. It was like walking into a museum of Indian history. They had a beautiful glass top coffee table full of arrow heads and picture frames on the walls with the same along with other Indian artifacts. They brought out several coffee cans full of old coins and arrow heads that they had found and collected over the years.

The next day of our visit, we all got up early, ate breakfast, and Herman took us way back to the mountains to show us where and how to look for arrow heads. We had so much fun and even found a few that day, so we had quite the collection of souvenirs to share with everyone back home and it hadn't cost us a dime. We learned some interesting history about the Indians of Wyoming from Bernice and Herman.

As it often happens on travels, we needed to do some laundry. Bernice had an old clothes wringer she used to wring out the clothes before hanging them to dry. I was not paying attention as Candace and I were pulling the clothes through the wringer, and my arm went right into the wringer along with the shirt. I let out a scream and Candace yelled. Then came the posse. The moms unplugged the wringer and released the rollers. My poor arm looked like one of those cartoon characters that get flattened by a roller compactor. My arm turned black and blue clear down to my fingers. Luckily, I didn't break anything, but it sure felt like I did. I remember my poor arm looked so deformed from the elbow down.

Bernice put together a remedy to soak my arm in, then wrapped it with a thin Ace bandage soaked in the solution. My mom gave me some aspirin. After a while, my arm didn't hurt as much, later that day it turned back to a normal looking arm, although still black and blue. When I do something, I always find myself in the same pickle. At least I did not have to go to the emergency room or cause our trip to be cut short like so many times before. I know that was what was going through everyone's minds.

We had a wonderful time visiting Wyoming and learned a lot of history too. As we pulled away from Bernice and Herman's, the song, "Home on the Range," came to mind. Yes, that's exactly where Bernice and Herman lived, a place where the buffalo roam and the deer and the antelope play. We saw all that wildlife while we were there.

After our wonderful vacation, my dad surprised us that following Saturday with a day trip to the Winchester Mystery House in San Jose, which isn't far from our hometown. Penny and I were so excited. There again, one place combined the history and mystery I was so fascinated with.

Mrs. Winchester had been the heir to the Winchester rifle fortune that her husband started. They never had any children. There is such an interesting story behind this woman and the building of her mansion. It showcases her mysterious way of thinking and her reliance on psychic mediums to guide her on building this enormous Victorian mansion.

We were told in the beginning of the tour not to wonder off because it could take some time to find us. Since doors opened into walls and stairways led to nowhere, I could see how one could get trapped and not be found for quite a while. I was in total awe. We all were really fascinated with the switchback staircase, which has forty-four steps that rise only about nine feet since each step is only two inches high. This was to accommodate Mrs. Winchester's severe arthritis. Mrs. Winchester believed that all the people who were killed by the Winchester rifle would haunt her, so she was told by mediums to keep building her house in a way to keep all their spirits away.

After the tour, as my family and I headed back home and shared our thoughts on this adventure, my mind focused on how lucky and blessed my sister and I were for having our great family.

That following week I was back at my volunteer job as a candy striper at the hospital, telling all the patients, I came in contact with about my adventures to Utah, Wyoming, and the Winchester Mystery House. Life could have not been better with all my adventures and taking care of sick people and sharing my life's experiences with them.

Chapter 9

High School Years

fter junior high going through my yearbook reading what comments of me that had been shared, and what others had to say, including teachers and school staff. For the most part, everything made me smile. I kind of wondered if all those comments were true words or fake. I soon turned my attention forward, getting prepared for new beginnings and entering a young adult world of four years with so many changes of life sure to follow.

High school starts out with everybody realizing everyone has changed. It seemed like the minute we hit high school we were in for the rollercoaster ride of our lives. Freshman year is just about settling in and juggling all six classes you have with homework and projects. You find out you have no time for fun or your friends as much as you did before, except if you had PE, Home Economics, or lunch time together. Freshman year is simply about adjustment.

I still was that shy, freckled-face girl, but I did start to come out of my shell somewhat. I did have that reserve side, except for this one time in my freshman year when I exposed a side of me, I didn't even know existed. From what I remember, it was around the beginning of the year and my first period class was math with Mr. Oui (pronounced "we") a very soft spoken, Asian man who had a gentle soul. His dress code was the same every day. He always wore slacks, a nice shirt with a tie, and those horrible "Mr. Magoo" glasses that were very popular with adults back then. Mr. Magoo was a cartoon character back in my younger years.

I was sitting in Mr. Oui's class trying to pay attention because math was not one of my best subjects. Out of the blue, this guy sitting behind me, who had always picked on me throughout grade school and junior high, started bothering me. I do recall his name however will just call him Richard. I think his antics was his way of showing me he liked me. The thing of it was I didn't like him.

While Mr. Oui continued writing math problems on the board, Richard kept pulling my bra strap and snapping it. On about the sixth snap, I turned around and let him have it with a great big backhand. It knocked him right out of his desk, and he landed against the bookcase, sitting there dazed while everyone laughed. Mr. Oui tried to control the situation. You could tell he was very frustrated and could not believe someone like me could have done such a thing. For the remaining period, Richard was moved to the back of the room.

After class, Mr. Oui, had both Richard and I stay to find out what had taken place and to apologize to each other. I wasn't too keen on apologizing to someone who was always picking on me, but I guess I had hurt Richard's pride, which I thought he deserved for that and all the other times before.

As I told my side of the story, Richard made all these faces and sarcastic remarks. Believe it or not, Mr. Oui had heard enough of him and told him to go to his other class and that he would deal with him later. After Richard left, Mr. Oui remarked for me to go ahead and go, he didn't want me to be late for my next class. As I headed out the door, he called out, "Hey, Sandie." As I turned around, he gave me a thumbs up. I felt so good at that time. For once I had a teacher who defended me rather than stand against me. It is a good feeling to know you are not always wrong like some make you out to be.

As time went on through high school, I had some great times and made a lot of friends. When you become a teen, that's when you start to learn a lot about people and situations. For example, friends are not always true, and adults are not always who they seem. I believe a lot of people out there can relate or are going through the same thing. Like I said before, I was such a quiet, shy, keep-to-myself kind of person who got hurt easily, and you get taken advantage of more when you are this type of person but only by those who are vindictive, manipulative, and down and out mean.

When you are pushed by these types of people, it does open up your bolder side. Sometimes this can be a not-so-good thing, depending on how you handle it, because when you let things build up inside you lose all control. When you do explode, everyone thinks you are the bad guy. So, I guess being the quiet, shy person does have its advantages despite its disadvantages. It allows us to control our temperament in a different way to those who come against us. You eventually learn that when you are surrounded by those who are strong individuals with meanness in them. However, I had such a big heart for others who were bullied or made fun of. I know there were a few kids in high school I became friends with that others made snide remarks about. I guess it was because I knew what it felt like to be hurt.

I think when we are going through hurts and trials, especially myself, I believe we are being molded into who we later become. That's why God gives us a free will. He doesn't choose our paths; He lets us decide and then guides us if we truly seek Him. But I was not seeking God at this point as a teenager. I only knew of Him through my family members who followed His Word. However, I know God started working in me at a very early age. I always felt something different about myself. I do believe God tugged on my heart strings a lot.

I found myself getting caught up in so much drama with individual people. One minute, I was Saint Sandie and the next, I was Easily Persuaded Sandie by all the peer pressure we all go through. I guess you will understand more of me being Saint Sandie and peer pressured Sandie as you read on.

My penchant for defending the underdog led me to become friends with some exceptionally nice, down-to-earth girls. In fact, these two friends were true Christians, which is unusual for being a teen in high school. They were true people and never fake like most. You know how peer pressure is growing up; you always had to fit in or do what everyone else does. If not, you were teased and made fun of. And that's exactly what happened with these two girls. I do remember their names but will call them Lisa and Maria instead.

Maria was more outspoken. She was always happy and smiling and always funny. Don't get me wrong, she also had her down moments like we all do, and she found herself getting caught up with peer pressure as well and really tried hard to not let it consume her. Lisa, on the other hand, was very shy with a reserved spirit and was a very proper dresser. She always wore skirts and blouses with a sweater, never any jewelry but a watch, and no make-up of any kind. She was a bit tall and large-boned and had long blonde hair. She was not thin, but her size fit her height and bone structure. And she had a heart of gold with such strong faith. We became good friends and even had a couple of classes together.

I can remember her crying because of the pressure on her. You could see the hurt on her face and hear it in her voice. But she always told me she would go somewhere secretly and pray; she then would feel so much better. I truly knew how she felt because her and I were so much alike, except I was not a Christian like she was. But something told me to keep asking and listening to these two wonderful girls. I asked a lot of questions about their beliefs. They always pressed on no matter what the enemy threw at them.

Even though they both had strong faith, they did not go around preaching or anything like that, but their actions told of their faith. They both were very humble and had such gentle and kind spirits. These two girls were very special to me. God must have sent them my way so I could learn and know more about my inner self. And now that I am an adult, I can see that is exactly what the Lord was doing.

My time in high school continued to teach me a lot about people, including who to trust and who not. My first experience of a very upsetting time was with my close friend, Alice. She and her sister and brother were going through a rough time as their parents were going through a divorce. I believe there was other things going on with her parents that she would not mention. I could relate to what was going on in her family because we had family members who were going through divorces and I had seen the hurt the kids went through.

Alice came to me and told me she had met this guy who was quite a bit older than her. She explained they were going to go down to L.A. to be together. I remember being really scared for her, and I told her she was making a big mistake for them both. She begged me to not tell anyone, including her parents. She made me promise and told me that if I was such a great and true friend, I would keep this quiet and act like I didn't know anything. I promised her I would. Who would have known this would lead to something a lot more than pretending?

This was my first experience with trying to remain a true and faithful friend. Such agony and hurt happened with Alice and her family. Since we were such good friends, her parents suspected I knew something. Alice had been gone for about four days before I was confronted by her parents and the police at my home. I will never forget the horrible feeling I felt when they came to my door and my dad answered it. The look on my dad's face! He was angry, mad, and scared all at the same time. I knew then I was in deep trouble.

My mom looked at me and said I'd better do some fast talking. When Alice's dad and mom begged me, and her mom was crying, I couldn't take it anymore. I was so pressured by them, my folks, and the cops, I broke down and bawled my head off. The police said I would be arrested if I had information and lied about it. I remember feeling sick to my stomach, like I was going to throw up, because of the fear and guilt I felt.

Just then, something inside of me took hold and I started to feel calm. I heard this voice telling me to speak the truth and it will be ok. My mind had been spinning in all different directions when it finally came to a halt. I recalled what Lisa and Marie shared with me all the time about being honest and truthful. Sometimes it seems like a lie is the better way out, but the enemy makes you feel that way. It is the truth that sets you free.

I proceeded to tell them everything I knew at that time. I felt so much better, even if it meant me losing a friend. I remember Alice's mom giving me a big hug and thanking me for finally telling the truth. After the L.A. police were notified, it took a while to locate Alice and that guy. I prayed every night at bedtime that Alice would be safe, to please find her and bring her home, and to comfort her family and to let them stay together.

Los Angeles is a big place so there was a lot of ground to cover. I gave the police a description of the van that Alice left in. Vans were the thing of the '70s, so it was going to be like finding a needle in a haystack for sure. As the days and weeks passed, my mom and Alice's mom kept in touch along with the police to see if there were any new leads. It took weeks for Alice and her boyfriend to be located, but once they were found, it was a happy ending for Alice's folks and mine. But I truly lost a friendship. Sometimes in certain situations I guess promises are meant to be broken. Especially if the situation could be a dangerous one.

It took a very long time for Alice and I to gain a semi-friendship back. She told me I would never be a trusted friend. My heart hurt so bad at being told that. Didn't she even realize what pressure I was under with her folks and mine as well as the police? I tried to explain it to her, but she didn't want to hear anything I had to say. I felt so torn because I thought I did what was right and then I got punished for maybe saving her life.

I went to my two spiritual friends, Lisa and Maria, and asked them, what should I do. They both told me to pray about it, and that God was in control of the whole situation. Then they both grabbed my hands and we bowed our heads. When I closed my eyes, I heard the sweetest prayer coming from these two wonderful angels who I was blessed to have as my friends. After they prayed with me, we embraced in a hug. I felt so much better and a peace came over me.

But this wasn't the first or the last time friendships became broken in my world, No, this was only the beginning of troubled friendships for me.

Chapter 10

Our Horrifying
Camping Trip

s I look back on being a young girl and teen growing up, I can see where God and the enemy played a big part in my life as they both do in each and everyone's. I was always getting into predicaments. For example, even in the midst of our great family trips, chaos took place that mostly was due to me getting hurt or having reactions to something I had come in contact with. It was always something with me, all the time! I thought either God was mad at me about something or the devil wanted me and my family to always, be in turmoil.

For example, I had another serious mishap on one of our camping journeys. One night, everyone decided to build a big campfire to roast marshmallows. All of us kids went around and picked up a bunch of wood and twigs so we could have a big fire. We used some of the twigs to roast marshmallows. As the night grew, we put the fire out and everyone headed to bed.

The next morning, I woke up with my face feeling weird. My throat was itching and hurt at the same time. My eyes were almost swollen shut. I cried out to my mom. She jumped up, took one look at me, and yelled out in fear. I remember how weird my body felt. I was swollen from head to toe. My mom felt sick to her stomach; she then ran to the outhouse bathroom.

As she was vomiting, she lost her dentures in the outhouse toilet. She screamed for my dad, and not only did he come running, but everyone else in our group as well. When they all arrived, there my mom stood with her hand over her mouth bawling and pointing at the toilet yelling that her teeth fell into it. My dad instantly said, "Well don't think for one minute I am crawling down there to get your teeth no matter how many payments I have to make for a new set." For such a quiet man, he made it very clear that he was not going to retrieve her blankety-blank teeth. Of course, Mom wasn't expecting him to retrieve them either.

Here again, we had to cut our trip short and come home after only three days. That weekend, my body disfigured grotesquely, and my poor mom kept her mouth covered with a scarf the whole time until she was able to get to the dentist. Mom was just totally beside herself with her missing teeth and my deformity. What a team we were! And since the insurance was not that good, it made for one heck of an expensive trip.

That Monday, my mom took me to our family doctor. Dr. Hawley was a wonderful man and good doctor. He met us at the back door of his office because, I looked so bad he didn't want to scare the other patients in the waiting room. To let you know how disfigured my face was, well, if you have ever seen the movie *Mask*, starring Cher, that's real close to how my face looked.

Dr. Hawley questioned my mom about our camping trip and asked if we remembered me going on a hike or standing next to some foliage. I informed him we picked up a bunch of twigs and wood to burn in our campfire. He then asked me if there were leaves on anything that I picked up, I told him "Yes, we picked up a bunch of twigs with leaves and used them to start the fire for our marshmallow roast." He then said he believed, I came in contact with poison oak and had a severe allergic reaction to its burning and inhaling the smoke. He told me I would have been better off touching it rather than burning it since ingesting is the worst.

By looking at me, I could say it certainly was. I had it inside my mouth, everywhere. Dr. Hawley told us I had the worst case possible, the worst he had ever seen. Dr. Hawley knew my folks were on a very tight budget and did not have good medical insurance, so he did everything possible to keep me from being hospitalized. However, he told my folks that if I started having trouble breathing or the swelling got worse, he would have no choice but to admit me to the hospital. I had to go to the doctor's three times a week for shots and bathe in this solution every night. I truly believed my face would never be normal again. I also remember how the inside of my body felt. It was out of place and inflamed.

I missed a whole month of school. My mom retrieved my assignments, and friends from school who lived near also brought my homework as well. I'm sure it was to see how disfigured I was. My healing was a slow and long process, but my family and I made it through. Months went by and one day my mom ran into Dr. Hawley at the store. The first thing he said was, "How has Sandie been? She hasn't been around any poison oak lately?" My mom laughed and said we were extra careful about everything when it came to shrubbery.

It took my folks awhile to pay off my poison oak bill and my mom's new dentures. Of course, once certain bills were paid, that old devil would kick us down again. The last payment to Dr. Hawley made my mom so happy. I remember that day; she had picked my sister and I up from school. She was in such a great mood because this was a day to rejoice and be glad in it. We went into the office to pay the bill off and my mom had such a big smile on her face, like she had just won a prize.

On our way out the door, I asked if we could get an ice cream cone, which she agreed, as long as it, didn't spoil our dinner. We were in heaven. What could be more exciting than getting a bill paid off and ice cream from our favorite place.

Thrifty Drugs had the best ice cream ever. We were focused on what flavor of ice cream we were going to pick. As I stepped up into our truck, I put my hand right on the frame of the door to push myself up. Of course, the unthinkable happened. That's right, I slammed the door shut, right onto my thumb. I let out this blood curdling scream, and my sister was yelling. Mom jumped out of the truck and ran over to open the door. I remember her yelling and crying, saying, "Oh my God, Sandie, now I have to work on another bill!" "Looks like no ice cream for us today," my sister yelled. We marched back into Dr. Hawley's office to see what damage I had done to my smashed thumb. Turns out, I had sprained it. Dr. Hawley put a splint on it free of charge. Because of that, we ended up getting ice cream after all. At least there was some calm over the storm for my folks at that moment anyway.

My sister and I were always getting hurt somehow. But I was the one that the devil picked on the most. In our younger years, Penny and I suffered from bad allergies to pollen and whatever else was in the air. There again came swollen, itchy eyes and a lot of sinus drainage. We had to have shots all the time during that season, and, of course, I had a little extra allergy added to it. I was highly allergic to dust, so every time my mom cleaned, I had to leave the house. Plus, she had to wash my bedding more than usual. I did outgrow this dust allergy, but not the others. My mom was happy I had outgrown the dust allergy so I could join in the cleaning. She may have been thrilled, but I wasn't.

Chapter 11

My Powder Blue Love Bug and the Jobs I Needed to Keep

ost teenagers can hardly wait until they turn sixteen so they can take driver's ed class and get their licenses. I can remember my driver's ed class and the movies we had to watch. They were meant to scare us so bad that we would hopefully be extra cautious drivers. To me, they were like watching a real-life horror show. After all that horror of watching people being decapitated in some major accident, you left feeling so overwhelmed about dying in a car. It really scared me about wanting to drive.

Then a new movie came out on the big screen by Disney called *Herbie The Love Bug*. Herbie is 1963 Volkswagen Beetle, a character that was featured in several Disney motion pictures over the years. This Volkswagen Beetle has a mind of its own and is capable of driving itself. It is also a serious contender in auto racing competitions. Herbie is distinguished by red, white, and blue racing stripes from his front to back bumper; a racing-style number "53" on the front luggage compartment lid, doors, and engine lid; and a yellow-on-black '63 California license plate.

After seeing this movie, I became excited about driving and having an adventure just like Herbie and his crew. I remember leaving the theater with a couple of my closest friends talking about how great it would be to have a cool Beetle Bug like Herbie. The days and months went by until I finished my driver's ed class to venture into driver's training. Wahoo! I was excited I passed!

Now it was onward down to the DMV for the big driving test to get my actual license. I was so nervous and ecstatic at the same time. I know my folks were just as nervous as we drove down to the center. It seemed like hours went by while we waited for them to call me back, I was getting so nervous my stomach started hurting. Then I heard this deep voice from behind the counter say, "Sandra Hann, please step up to the counter." It made me think of my piano teacher calling to me as I would approach at one of my recitals.

I remember my dad saying, I would be fine and to remember all he had taught me. The thing of it was I was so nervous with my stomach hurting I did not remember a thing my dad had taught me. Then it came to me! Was my dad telling me, I was not only going to be tested on my driving, but on changing a tire and checking the oil too? That changed everything for me. Then my parents put me at ease, saying, "No, just driving."

Yes, my dad told my sister and I, if we were going to drive and have a vehicle, we needed to know how to change a tire and check our fluids, and most importantly, know how to put gas in and know how to read the gas gauge so we knew when to fill up. So, yes, that was what I was thinking when they called me back for my driver's test. Not just driving but all the above. I could handle the driving part.

As I pulled away with this instructor, he began giving directions with his stern voice, "Turn right here, turn left here, now parallel park." I could not help but glance out of the corner of my eye and notice him putting a check mark each time I would stop, park, turn, or hit my blinker. I just knew it was going to be bad, and that they were all probably black marks and I was going to fail. "Man," I thought, "this guy does not cut any slack by the movement of his pen." When I returned to the DMV and walked inside, my folks asked how I did. I answered, "Well, I don't know, but by the movement of the instructor's pen, I don't think I did very well." My dad's famous words were, "Just wait and see."

When my name was called by the lady behind the counter, my heart just sank. I just knew I would have to retake the driver's test again, at a later date. In that instant, as that lady behind the counter peered down through her black framed glasses, my mind wondered back to when I practiced so hard for my piano recitals and failed because of being nervous, and then my piano teacher peering down at me through her glasses. At the window, I spoke first, saying, "When can I come back and retake my driver's test again?" The woman looked down at me and smiled as she said, 'Well, young lady." By the sound of her voice when she said that, I knew I was doomed. She then enlightened me with, "It looks like you won't have to come back because you passed."

"Oh my gosh, are you sure! I mean you didn't get me mixed up with someone else, did you?"

"Nope," she said as I was jumping up and down yelling. My mom and dad were excited for me, but my dad was getting a little nervous at the scene I was causing, so he asked me to calm down.

I immediately asked if I could drive home, and of course they said yes! But it turned into having a back seat and front seat driver telling me to watch out for that car, the light is red, slow down, speed up a little, you have a stop sign. They sounded like my driver instructor. I think I made a big mistake by asking to drive home. When we pulled up in the driveway and I put the car into park, turning the ignition off, I think my folks were expecting me to say, "Well, how did I do?" But I tricked them both by saying, "Ok, we are here, and I got us all here in one piece. Aren't you proud?" After that, I was always asking my mom or dad if they needed anything from the store. Most of the time it was yes.

My folks had said they would help my sister and I get started on our first car, but we had to have a job so we could pay for our insurance and the vehicle's upkeep. I immediately looked for a job. I babysat most of the time for some neighbors up the street. Most of my jobs were babysitting for people around our neighborhood. I kept saving my money so I would have enough to put into my first car and plus get my insurance.

One day I was looking out the living room window, when my dad drove up in this little Volkswagen Bug. I knew it was for me. I ran outside and my dad threw me the keys. It was powder blue with a crank sunroof and red seats, very clean, and the body was in excellent shape. My dad had bought it from a guy that he worked with who had used it for college. I was so eager to drive it. It was a stick shift, so I had to learn the gears before I drove. As my dad took me out to learn the gears, my mind would drift back to the Love Bug movie. How awesome I had a car so similar. I knew it did not drive itself, and it was never in races, but this little Love Bug of mine could and would take me everywhere on such limited gas and park into the tightest of spaces.

Now I was able to go to more places for my job hunting. I first got another babysitting job for the summer and the place was just around the corner from my Aunt Glenda and Uncle Al. After I was done babysitting for the day, I would pop in and visit with them. The family I babysat for was an older couple who had kids later in life, and they were not kid-ori-entated people. He had his own vending machine business, so he was always gone, and she worked at a hardware store. It was kind of sad because, on her days off, she always called her employer and asked if they needed her for that day. She couldn't even handle her own kids, so she worked to get away from them.

After watching their kids during that summer, I can see why these people were always so eager to work. The children had no discipline; they were total monsters for sure. Their ages were seven, five, and three. One day while watching these little monsters, I was making lunch when I heard a loud banging like someone hammering something. The banging was coming from Tony's room. I tried opening his bedroom door, but he had it locked. I yelled for him to unlock the door, of course his answer was the same as most kids his age, which was, "No." So I ran outside to peer through his bedroom window. I could not believe what I saw. Tony was nailing blankets to his wall. I yelled at him to open the door or I was going to call his mom, but his response was very similar to what most kids would say today: "Oh, that's ok, my mom doesn't care. "

As I made my way back into the house, I walked in to find Danielle doing her ballet on the back of the couch and the little one running around the living room and back down the hall with a trail of toilet paper following him through every room. I stood there in total amazement on how these three children were running amuck. I got myself together and yelled out really loud, "Ok you three, that is it. I have had enough." I made Danielle and the little one clean up all the toilet paper, which they had to do before they could eat their lunch. I also yelled through the door that if Tony wanted to eat lunch, he was to remove all those blankets and come out to the table to eat. After a few attempts in coxing him out, he finally opened his door. I couldn't believe what I saw looking at his wall with huge nails the blankets were attached to. I remember saying to him, "Oh my God, Tony, your mom is going to be so mad at both of us." He just grinned and said to me, "Don't worry, Sandie. My mom probably won't even notice."

After that, my babysitting days ended with that family. Six months was way too long with that bunch. I thought to myself, "Wow, I don't think I ever want any children in the future after all that turmoil with those three."

It wasn't much later when I found a job doing something I really loved and enjoyed. I was hired on at Merle Norman Cosmetics. The shop was upstairs in this little strip mall downtown. Holly, the owner, and her husband was a school teacher. They had no children, but they had two Scottish terriers that were their kids. She would bring them to the shop sometimes. They were so cute when they were groomed and had plaid bows in their ears.

Holly and I had a fun and friendly relationship. She had a lot of confidence in me and would leave me in charge when school was out during the summer to open the shop while she was on vacation. I took care of it like it was my own. I loved doing facials and makeup. There is something about when you are down or do not feel very pretty, it's amazing what a little makeup can do to lift your spirits. Holly even had me go over to San Francisco to makeup models for fashion shows. That was a lot of fun.

That was the one job I truly enjoyed. But I had to keep up on my school work. Holly was a real stickler on that. She told me if I got behind or my grades started to drop, she would not let me work until things were brought back up to where they were supposed to be. My folks said the same thing. One day, I decided to cut school with some friends, which was the first time for me. You can bet I got caught. My folks were livid. They took it, to extreme; one that was over the top. (For some reason, my folks always were extreme with my punishment). I thought they would ground me from my car for a while or from being around my friends. But what they did was so hurtful. They told me I had to quit my job with Merle Norman and for me to call Holly to let her know, I was not able to work for her anymore because I cut school.

I called her and told her; I was crying so hard. She even came over to the house and tried to talk to my folks. But the answer was still no. I was totally crushed. I occasionally came by to visit her even though I couldn't work for her anymore. She sometimes had me house-sit for a weekend if her and hubby went somewhere.

I had to look for another job because I had insurance and gasoline to pay for. About a month after leaving Merle Norman, I got a job working at Lord's Ice Cream Parlor. That was an ok job, but nothing like working at Merle Norman. From the ice cream parlor, I switched to working at JC Penny's in the catalog dept. It paid little bit more than the ice cream place. The store manager and his wife were good friends with my folks. I didn't mind working for JC Penny's, but I truly did miss Merle Norman. I can remember my folks telling me that if I ever cut school again, I would have to give up any job, and my car would be put on hold. Yes, my folks were strict with me.

It was Christmas time and all of us co-workers at JC Penny's festively decorated our stations. Mr. Bower, the store manager, had some poinsettias delivered and he put one in our break room. That day, one of the girls and I were having lunch and I read the little tag on the poinsettia. It warned the plant was poisonous and to keep it away from children and animals. Being the Curious George that I was (and still am), I took a little tiny piece no bigger than the end of my fingernail and proceeded to chew it and spit it back out. No more than seconds after doing so, my tongue and lips started to swell, and I couldn't talk very well. My tongue was about three to four times its actual size and my lips looked like a bad Botox job. Of course, Botox was non-existent back then, but it is just something for comparison.

My co-worker ran to get our supervisor, who ran and got the store manager. My folks were away for the weekend, so my supervisor drove me to the ER. Mr. Bower went back to work and told me to go home when finished up at the hospital, and if I needed an extra day off, it was ok. But before he left, he was very stern in asking me why I had done such a thing. I was crying and, with my fat tongue and ugly big lips, I tried to explain I just wanted to see what would happen, but no one could understand me very well. The first thing the doctor asked was if I swallowed any. I told him I had just taken a couple of chews and spit the petal out. He told me I was very lucky. I had an angel watching over me because it could have been worse and caused a whole lot of other damage, like make my insides swell where I would not be able to breath. I could have possibly died.

When my parents returned home and found out what had happened, my mother was so angry with me. I thought that if the poinsettia didn't kill me, she was. I really made her German blood boil that time. But she and everyone had a good reason to be angry with me. I really deserved what I had received for being such a dummy and for doing something so stupid.

I really don't know why I tried something so off the wall, but I did find out that being curious is not always a good thing. It can either kill you or make you out to be such a fool. So please, please, please, if there are any Curious Georges out there reading this, do not, and I repeat do not, let your curiosity tempt you. Think it through and consider the outcome. I am living proof of doing curious things and it never turns out to be good.

The ER doctor ended up giving me a shot, observed me for a while, then sent me home. After that whole ordeal, which was no laughing matter on my part, my co-workers constantly reminded each other to put the poinsettias up out of reach from Sandie. Mr. Bower even made comments that he didn't think he should order anymore poinsettias for decoration because he had someone who liked to sample them. I was the laugh for a very long time, but I had that coming and deserved those remarks, I guess.

As time went by, I slowly spiced my Love Bug up. I put awesome wheels on it, got some cool seat covers, filled my ashtray with hard candies, and put a no smoking sign on the passenger sun visor. None of my friends smoked; neither did I. Everyone knew I did not allow smoking in my car, so for the smokers, when they would open my ashtray and grab a candy, they would forget about lighting up.

One of the adventures I had with my Bug was with my best friend, Shannon. She and I went to the Castlewood Country Club her folks belonged to and met her mom for lunch one afternoon. After lunch, Mrs. Ashworth, who was a big tennis buff, was going to play a few rounds of tennis with friends, while Shannon, me, and my Love Bug were going to drive around Castlewood and look at all the beautiful homes.

The Pink Palace stood out amongst them all. You could see it sitting up on the hilltop when you were driving below on the freeway. We both had always wanted to see it up close and wondered who lived there.So here we were driving and looking in awe at these luxurious homes, when all of a sudden, right in front of us was the Pink Palace.

It was surrounded by high cement walls the same color as the house with a huge double drive through solid gate. The color was not bright pink; it was like an adobe sand color with a slight pink tinge to it. I guess you would say it was a Mediterranean-style mansion. I told Shannon I was going to pull up to the gate so we could stand on the hood of the car and take a peek. As we were standing there trying to be quiet and discreet, we heard the gate opening. We both were really scared. Shannon jumped down while I was still standing on the hood of the car hanging on the gate. All of a sudden, a man's voice came from around the corner of the gate and said, "Can I help you girls?" We didn't know what to say, but Shannon spoke up and said, "Yes, we have always admired this home from the freeway and we just wanted to see what it looked like up close."

We then apologized for hanging on his gate. He smiled, then asked if we would like to come in and take an even closer look around. Of course, we did! When we stepped through the gate, our mouths just dropped. The grounds were absolutely beautiful. Back then we didn't know who Thomas Kinkaid was, and he probably didn't have famous paintings then, but I would compare our host's landscaping to one of his beautiful garden paintings. In the center of the garden was a beautiful swimming pool you walked around to enter the doors to the house's entrance. Our host opened the door and we walked into an entry way with a floor of beautiful marble. To the right of us was a beautiful, garden mural painted on the wall that had a fountain of beautiful, real running water falling into this pond.

To the left of us, you stepped down into a huge sunken living room where we saw an elderly lady sitting with a big smile on her face. The gentleman introduced her as his wife and told her how he met us. We were so embarrassed, but they were very nice about the whole thing. They gave us a tour of this remarkable home. What was even more unique with this couple was that they had a specific name for every room in the house.

The first stop was the kitchen; it was huge, very cheerful, and I am sure every women's dream. It was a very pale pink with white cabinetry, and it reminded me of cotton candy. And guess what the kitchen was named? Yes, they called it the Cotton Candy Kitchen.

Next, we preceded down a long hall with tons of family pictures and into these beautiful bedrooms. The first bedroom was the master and it was called the Peacock Room. It was gigantic, and its beauty was in the most exquisite use of colors. They were all the shades of a peacock. The ceiling had a mural of a peacock with its body and feathers lined with jewels. There was rubies, turquoises, amethysts, jade, and gold. When the overhead light was flipped on, the whole ceiling lit up like a beautiful, stained glass church window.

The next room was called the Safari Room and had African wildlife pictures on the walls. It was done up in zebra and leopard decor. We proceeded to the Floral Room, which was decorated with floral wallpaper and elegant pictures of gardens, and it boasted flower arrangements on the dresser and a small table. There was also a library and study. There were so many rooms.

As we proceeded to leave this extraordinary mansion, we both gave them a gracious hug and thanked them for giving us a tour. They invited us to stop by anytime to visit. We were in such awe that they would invite us back. What wonderful people they were. I learned that not all rich people are bad.

About a month or so went by and we were out of school for summer vacation. Shannon and I decided to head up to Castlewood County Club to have lunch, and pay a visit to our new found friends who had asked us to come by anytime. After we had lunch, we piled into my Love Bug and headed to the hacienda mansion. Upon our approach, there were two men in suits with guns standing outside the gate. When we stopped, they approached the car and asked us how they could help us. We knew immediately something big had happened. Who else would stand out in front of a huge mansion gate in suits with guns? I explained we had visited the couple about a month ago and the owners had said we could stop by anytime to visit, and here we were. One gentleman, who was on my side of the car said, "Well, young ladies, it looks like you will not be visiting today. One of them has passed away." We were sorry to hear that.

As we drove off, I told Shannon maybe we could find out which one had passed and send a card. The next day, it came out in the *Livermore Herald* newspaper that there had been a sudden death in the Castlewood Country Club Hacienda. As I read on, I was astounded to learn, the gracious couple were related to the Hearst family. I immediately called Shannon and told her who it was. Once I told her, she let out this slight scream. We, of all people, had met someone of high importance.

Once we found out all the info, Shannon and I sent a sympathy card to the family with a little note attached and our signatures. We never received a reply back, and I really don't know if they received it. But what I do know is that Shannon and I had the most awesome experience two teens could ever have.

So, as this chapter comes to a close, I can honestly say no matter how good or bad the peer pressure of my teen life was, there was something about being able to jump in my car and take a long drive, just me and my Love Bug. And that, made everything better.

Chapter 12

Life with Intel and Murder in My Hometown

y last year of high school, I worked at Intel, the company that made chips and parts for almost all types technology back then. I really loved working there and met a lot of great people. It was there I had another experience with getting hurt physically and mentally.

Everything started out well at Intel. My best friend, Kari, and I were so excited the day we applied for the job, and even more so when we found out that both of us got it. It was our very first "real job" where you were paid well and had great benefits.

It was quite the experience working with machinery. About four months into the job, I was doing what I usually did in my little corner in a room filled with other machinery and others. Here again, I was curious like the time I tried the poinsettia. I was watching this metal slider that held these real thin wafer chips slide back and forth as it dropped these wafers into another part of the machine.

I was seriously watching it, bending over to look closer and studying how this piece of equipment worked, when my tweezer fell into this deep hole where the slider slid back and forth. I thought I would be quicker than the slider and reached in quickly to grab the tweezer as the platform went back. "I'll be the fastest tweezer drawer in the West," I thought. At that precise second, as I reached in fast to pull out the tweezer, the plate came back and bit my arm and held onto it.

I screamed, and my supervisor ran in, then called maintenance. I have never seen a team move so fast. They finally unstuck my arm. Thank goodness nothing was broken, though it turned a little black and blue before the night ended. They had me go and get my arm checked at the hospital. Thankfully, all was well.

The next day, I headed into work and everyone asked how my arm was. I told everyone it was nothing, it was fine and still attached. My supervisor sarcastically said, "Well, Sandra, you aren't the quickest draw yet, but maybe if you practice you might make it." I remember her and a few others laughing. I mustered up enough courage, then replied to her and her other laughing hyenas. "Your right, maybe I will keep practicing. I just know I can beat that machine." They all yelled at the same time and said "What! You're joking, right?" I smiled and said, "What do you think?" As I walked away, I thought to myself those women were such dorks.

I walked in the locker room and put on my gear, which consisted of nylon booties over your shoes, a snap-up nylon bunny suit, a nylon hood that tucked neatly into the collar so no hair showed, and, of course, these wonderful, huge safety glasses. Boy, were we styling! As my co-workers and I were gearing up in the locker room, one of the girls was talking about women who don't shave their legs or under their arms. My feisty side was still feeling a little quirky after the discussion about my quick draw practicing, so I came back with, "Well, I don't shave my arm pits. And when they get good and long, I braid them on special occasions." The look on their faces was priceless. One of them gave me a really heated look and said, "You're serious?" I said, "Yep, I'm serious. What do you think!" Boy, if that did not shut them up.

I knew these girls were going to talk about it to others, so I agreed with the ones who came up to me and asked the question by saying something like, "Who told you that silly story?" They would always say, "Oh Sandie, you are so bizarre." I always smiled and said, "Yes I am. You're just jealous because you aren't as bizarre as me." It really made people wonder about me, but, hey, I think it is good to let people wonder about you. Keep them guessing. It keeps all those troublemakers away from you because they don't know what to think.

My allergies were still horrible at this time. I had to give myself shots because they were so bad. I carried a small allergy syringe kit with me so I could give myself a shot in the thigh when I had an allergy attack, kind of like an Epie pen. Anyway, I was having an episode at work, so I went into the bathroom and gave myself a shot. Right when I did, one of those troublemaker girls walked in and immediately walked out. I knew exactly what she was going to do, and I was right. She had gone to the head supervisor and told her I was shooting up in the bathroom.

When I went back to the locker room to put my stylish gear back on, in came the supervisor with the chief of police and the department head (this woman was the biggest serpent of them all). She called me out like I was under arrest.

I walked out with the department manager to the department head's office. There they closed the door and told me I was going to be written up. My heart just sank. I have never been written up on any job I have worked. Our department manager was one mean son-of-a-gun. She didn't give me a chance to explain anything. They both assumed right then and there I was a druggy because one person saw and said so. There was a rumor going around which the gossipers, felt that explained why I reacted the way I did, when I stuck my arm into the machinery to retrieve my tweezer.

I left work feeling humiliated and betrayed. I went to my doctor's the next day and had him write me a note explaining the circumstance of my allergy kit. He wrote a very professional letter and included his number if there were any questions.

The next day when I went to work, everyone was staring at me like I had murdered someone. That is a horrible experience, walking into work and everyone is watching you like you are such a terrible human being. What was even worse was the ones who were staring at me the hardest were the ones really doing drugs. Isn't it ironic how the sayer is usually the doer? There were only a few who knew the truth. I marched right into the warden's office, or should I say Ms. Serpentine's office, and handed her the letter. Of course, she came back with some smart remark before even reading it. I walked out of her office and went to the locker room to get on my gear. Everyone was quiet, except for a few of my closest friends. We simply talked about what was going on that day.

When lunch break rolled around and we were heading to the lunchroom, Miss Witchy Poo walked by me with an angry look on her face. She did not even say a word, not even an apology. I knew she was angry because she was put on the spot with my doctor's note. It had made her look like such a fool, even though she was one. The whole time I worked there she never once said she was wrong or sorry, and neither did the supervisor or the snake that snitched on me.

Life at Intel went on. I had some who liked me and some who didn't, but that is ok because I had a few good friends still. One of them was Shawn. I will never forget him. He was gay, and very handsome I might add. He was a great friend. He had a fun personality and was very trustworthy. Of course, he too was talked about behind his back and made fun of because of who he was. Shawn, Kari, and I often had long conversations about his life and who he was. I never judged him, but even at that time I knew that what he or who he was trying to be was wrong. I once asked him if he really thought God made him that way. Shawn gave it some thought, and after a while he came back saying he did believe God made him that way for a reason. I don't know what that reason was.

I was not walking with the Lord at this time and I really and truly did not know much about God's Word, but what I did know in my heart was that God did not make Shawn to be a guy with feminine ways. I then said I knew God created women and men, not women to be like man and man to be like women. Shawn then asked Kari and I if he would go to hell for the way he was. Kari and I didn't really know the answer to that. We told Shawn to talk with a pastor and search for the real biblical truth.

A few more months rolled by and Intel had a big meeting to let us employees know that one of Intel's CEOs was flying in from Boston to look over how things were being run and our productivity. Naturally our head of the department, which we had many names for her, our most famous was Warden or Serpentine fire, made sure we knew that while the CEO was visiting, we were to be on our best behavior. At the time she said that, Shawn, Kari, and I looked at each other. She, of all people, defiantly needed to take her own advice.

The CEO from Boston arrived in our little farming town within the next couple of days. When I first saw him, he reminded me of the actor, Dudley Moore; he was the same height and size, but didn't have the English accent or Dudley's sense of humor. I recall when he was touring our stations, he stopped and talked to everyone about their jobs. When he came in my department, he made his way right to me and started talking about how he heard about my battle with my quick draw skills. I politely said, "Well, if you really would like to know about my quick reflexes with the machine, you might want to talk it over with my supervisor just so nothing is missed." At that moment, his face turned tomato red because he was embarrassed and so was I. How dare my supervisor discuss what happened with me to the CEO!

The weekend came, and Kari and I had made plans to take a drive to spend the day over in the Bay Area. When I came by to pick her up and waited for her to finish getting ready, Kari's cousin, Doug, came by in a very emotional state in tears. Kari's grandma asked what was wrong. Doug proceeded to let her know that something awful had happened that he was involved in, but he hadn't known at the time how far it was going to go; he was led to believe something different by his so called, friend, Jim. Doug had been totally deceived, and you could tell by his voice and his emotions.

Being a young teenager listening to his story, I too was in such disbelief on how the event happened. While Doug told his story, my heart just sank because, prior to hearing him, I remembered reading about the event in our town newspaper days before.

The truth finally came to pass as the story unfolded about this robbery gone wrong. Jim was a deacon in my aunt and uncle's church. Apparently, he was having an affair. So instead of going through all the proceedings of a divorce, Jim decided to murder his wife and fake a robbery to make it look like Mary had been murdered during the robbery. Jim told Doug that he needed extra cash for some debts, so if he made it look like a robbery, he then would be able to collect from his insurance company, he then would split it with Doug. Doug then asked, "What if your wife hears us and calls the police?" Jim told him that he would give her a sedative so she would sleep right through it.

Prior to the robbery taken place, Jim had told his in-laws that he and Mary were planning a weekend trip with just the two of them and wanted to know if the kids could spend the weekend. With everything arranged, he then dropped the kids off at the grandparents, went home, and later that night when Mary fell asleep, Jim suffocated her with a pillow, thinking she was truly dead. Then he phoned Doug to head over to carry onward with the robbery.

After the supposedly robbery had occurred, Doug left, and Jim waited awhile to call police to put his thoughts together. Later that night, he phoned the police, telling them he had just gotten home from a friend's, and discovered he had been robbed and he believed his wife had been murdered. When the police arrived, they immediately checked on Mary, felt for a pulse, and found a very faint one. They called for an ambulance.

On arriving at the hospital with Mary just barely alive, the police started questioning Jim. The hospital staff who were on duty with Mary's care found it odd that Jim would always ask if Mary had mentioned anything about the night of the robbery. Every time he walked in to see Mary and she heard his voice her monitors would go off. The staff really suspected something wrong and they made the report to the police. After about three days of Mary being on life support, she finally passed.

I couldn't even imagine what Jim and Mary's two children were going through knowing their dad had murdered their mom. How sad for Mary's family, and Jim's as well. It was a real shock to our community, especially since so many knew the family.

The outcome for Kari's cousin was not as bad as we thought it would be. Doug did get jail time for attempted burglary, and of course, Jim received quite a long sentence. It was the talk of the town for quiet sometime.

Further into my job at Intel, I met a new guy, Mark, who had just come on board. He was tall, had dark hair, and was very handsome. We became an item. He was my first true love. He lived in his grandmother's house on the next street over from where I lived. After work, we often got together to watch a movie or just sit and talk. Sometimes we hit the local Jack in the Box with some of our other friends. On occasion, we rode into work together. We really had a fun relationship, and I felt very comfortable around him. I wasn't anymore the lonely, shy Sandie who didn't have a boyfriend while everyone else did. I now could boast about my new, handsome guy.

After dating for a while, I was home one night and my folks were gone for the weekend. I was bored and wide awake after my shift, so I called Mark and asked him if he would mind having some company. He invited me to come over, and I told him I would be there in an hour. Of course, it took me that long to change my clothes and touch up my makeup and hair. Walking up the street, as I grew closer to Mark's, I noticed Kari's car parked in front of the house. "Why is she here?" The front door was open, and as I proceeded up the walkway, I could see through the screen. To my dismay, my best friend and my boyfriend were sitting next to each other on the sofa with his arm around her as he gave her a kiss.

My heart fell and I was so hurt. I thought, "How could he ask me to come over and not mention Kari was coming as well? "How could my best friend do that to me?" I was so betrayed and deceived by two people I cared for, and who I thought cared for me. How could they do this? I ran back home, my heart aching so bad it felt like someone had stuck a knife right through it. That was a hurt that I will never forget.

I had a good friend, Tommy, who was able to console me. Tommy was the boy next door, and we had been friends for a long time. He had joined the military, but we always wrote each other. When I told him what had happened, he told me he knew exactly how I felt because it had happened to him as well. He said it was an awful pain, but it teaches us to choose more wisely.

I felt so displaced and wondered who else was pretending to be my friend. My friend, Shawn, had moved and we kept in touch, but only for a short time. I always wondered if he did seek the truth about himself and find an inner peace. I wondered how Lisa and Marie reacted to things that were overwhelming and what they had to face being who they were. That made me stop and think maybe there was truth behind prayer. It always seemed to work for Lisa and Marie, but why wasn't prayer bringing me peace through my storms of life? I guess I just wasn't there yet with God.

I went back to work the next day and had nothing to say to Mark or Kari, Mark approached me and asked why I didn't come by last night. They both approached me and acted like nothing was wrong. I remember the anger in my voice and expression as I directed eye contact with both of them, and made the comment that they both were backstabbers and not friends of mine. I told them I didn't associate with evil, deceitful people who call themselves friends. I walked away and never said anything to either of them up till the time I left Intel.

I had been deciding for quite some time that I would like to move out of Livermore and go to college in Washington state. I truly loved Washington, and since I had family there, it seemed the place to go for new beginnings. My folks thought it was a good idea and a good place for a new start. It was the beginning of summer and my family had planned a trip to Hawaii with some of their friends. When we got back from our Hawaii trip, that was when I would make my big move to Washington state for college.

Chapter 13

Lime Green House on the Hill and the Cabin in the Woods

llow me to tell the story of the Lime Green House on the Hill. My grandmother and her husband, Don, who was my grandmother's third husband, lived in San Bruno located right next door to south San Francisco. They lived in a very nice home up on a hill where you could see the freeway below as well as an awesome view of south San Francisco. We went there often, and sometimes my sis and I would stay a weekend or a week during the summer.

My grandmother loved bright colors and lots of flowers, inside and outside. We never had a problem picking gifts for her; anything with bright colors or flowers made her happy. One weekend, Grandma called my mom beforehand and mentioned they painted the house. My mom asked, "What color did you choose?" My grandmother replied that the house was now very bright, and we would see it from the freeway with no problem. I remember my mom saying, "I hope it's not too off the wall, Mom. But I am sure we will spot it." Grandma's reply was, "Oh, you'll know once you get here." When she hung up the phone, I recall Mom saying, "I bet your grandma painted the house a bright yellow or lime green."

We were looking forward to Saturday morning and our trip over to grandma's. We couldn't wait to pick out her bright colored house on the hill. As we were heading down the freeway towards San Bruno, we all happened to look up the hill at the same time and in harmony we yelled out, "Oh my gosh!" Grandma wasn't kidding when she said we would be able to spot her home from the freeway. There stood the brightest, lime green structure you have ever seen. The color of grandma's house looked like a big neon sign.

Grandma and Don came out to greet us when we pulled up. My dad stepped out of the car, and with his favorite expression, said, "Holy Toledo! You weren't kidding Ma. That is one bright mess." Don also joined in and mentioned that the neighbors weren't too happy with it either. If Grandma liked it and was happy, that was all that mattered.

Our last visit in the Lime Green House on the Hill was when we were preparing for our trip to Hawaii. We stayed the night at Grandma's because she wasn't too far from the airport. It was there we were to meet some of mom and dad's close friends who were joining us. That night at Grandma's, we could hardly sleep because we were so excited to go to a place people only dream about. My high school friend Katie was going with us too. She and I stayed up most of the night talking about what we were going to wear, all the experiences we were going to have, and, let's not forget, all the cute island surfer dudes we were sure to meet. Oh yeah, we had it all planned out. Little did we know what was really in store for us. But I'll share more about the trip in the next chapter.

Soon my mom came downstairs to wake us up. We had to be at the airport by 7:00 a.m. I think Katie and I only got an hour or two of sleep, so we definitely were not going to be beauty queens on the plane or when we arrive in Honolulu. Katie complained that the way we looked we would probably attract all the not-so-cute guys. Mom and Granny came back with, "Oh, you girls are beautiful. You can catch up on your beauty rest on the plane."

I remember driving down the hill, waving back at Grandma and Don, not realizing it was to be our last family get together in the Lime Green House on the Hill. My grandmother and Don were moving to Pine Mountain by Yosemite National Park. They had told my folks the night we were there, but Penny and I didn't find out until we came back from our trip. My sis and I were really upset because we loved Grandma's house on the hill, even if it was lime green.

However, when we found they were going to be moving to a cabin in the woods, that was even better. All I could think about was the wildlife and what a wonderful place to be with nature. We headed up to Pine Mountain to see Grandma and help with some of the unpacking. I remember my first impression when we pulled up in front of their cabin home was that it was beautiful. I just loved it. It was in the heart of the forest. Deer would come down, and my grandmother said they got a lot of squirrels and raccoons. My sister and I were in seventh heaven the times we stayed with Grandma and Don on the weekends. We would put food out for the wild animals. What an adventurous place to be!

My grandmother and Don lived there for about a year. Don loved it, and so did we. But I guess it wasn't colorful enough for Grandma. I think she missed the Lime Green House. Plus, my grandmother was a very meticulous women and she always complained about sweeping up all the pinecones and pine needles that fell on the deck. She defiantly was not a nature kind of girl. I can remember my dad telling her that maybe if she painted the cabin lime green, it might keep all the animals away.

Penny and I weren't too happy with my grandmother moving from the mountain, but wherever Grandma lived, she always made it a fun place to visit. My grandmother's love of her family showed through her baked goods and big hugs. Yes, those were wonderful times spent, and I treasure the memories made in the Lime Green House on the Hill and in the Cabin in the Woods.

Chapter 14

Our Hawaii Adventure with Family and Friends

I wanted to remember every detail of my trip to Hawaii, so I decided to keep a journal of my adventures on the islands. As I write this chapter, I am looking back at my journal and re-living this chapter of my life all over again.

Our trip to Hawaii was my first time on a plane. The plane was a 747; we were on Flight 181. Looking out of the terminal window at this huge gigantic plane, I thought, "How is the size of that thing ever going to get off the ground?" Excited to start my journal, I wrote HAWAII in big bold lettering, to actually believe I was really going.

We had about a thirty-minute wait before boarding. I remember making a lot of restroom trips within that time because I was so excited and nervous. The first time on a plane has a way of making your bladder overreact and your stomach do all kinds of weird things, at least for me. I was journaling about my overactive bladder and my alien stomach gurgling when I heard this voice over the intercom say, "Now boarding Flight 181." Boy, did my stomach start feeling over anxious. My heart was fluttering, and I was thinking "Now I really have to go to the ladies' room!" My mom yelled "Sandra, you can't go now. You will miss the plane".

Stepping into the plane, I stood there in amazement. My breathing slowed down and my stomach went into a calm. The inside of the plane was not what I expected. It had three rows of seats across, it looked like I had stepped into a huge movie theater. My dad was telling me to keep walking because I was holding up everyone else trying to get seated. After we found our seats and everyone was all adjusted, we were ready for takeoff.

The captain came over the intercom and welcomed everyone aboard, inviting us to enjoy the flight to the wonderful islands of Hawaii. Then the stewardesses went through all the safety details, like how to use the oxygen masks and what to do in case of an emergency. Lastly, the flight attendants pointed out where the restrooms were. Just then, the captain came back on and said we were ready for takeoff and to sit back and relax. He told us once we were in the air, a light would come on to let us know we could unfasten our seat belts and walk around.

Katie, Penny, and I got to sit in the three seats by the window. Looking out as the plane picked up its momentum of speed, my heart was racing so fast. What a rush! How amazing to look out and see you are on the ground, and then next you are flying away from land and everything looks like one big dot, and then you see nothing but clouds.

I remember thinking wouldn't it be awesome, to actually see angels out on those clouds waving at us. At that instant, I knew if anything did happen while we are up in the air, we were closer to heaven. That thought made my plane ride more relaxing for me. As I sat back in deep thought, the light in front of the plane went off and the captain said we could now move around.

As soon as that light went off, all three of us girls jumped up and headed to the restroom. On our way there, to the rear of the plane, Katie and I checked out to see if there were any cute guys. We did see cuties, but they were already taken. As I entered this tiny hole-in-the-wall that was the restroom. Let me tell you something about those restrooms. First off, as big as that plane was, it had the tiniest bathroom I have ever been in. I thought our bathroom at home was small, but this one took the award for the smallest bathroom. Even an out-house had more room. These are extremely compact.

The first thing you had to figure out is how to use and even flush the toilet. Sitting there, I looked around to figure out how to use the sink and everything else. Like I said, this was no ordinary bathroom. It looked like something out of the futuristic Jetsons cartoon. The flight attendant should have given instructions on the restrooms as well, while she was instructing us all how to use all the other necessities available for emergencies. Isn't a bathroom for emergency use also?

I truly do not know how those women before me walked in and came out so quickly. Probably it was because they had flown many times and I am sure they had learned the restroom tricks I needed to figure out. When it came time to wash my hands, there were signs saying, "pull here, push here," so I was pulling and pushing but nothing was happening. They should have had arrows pointing to those things and not leave a person guessing the whole time.

When I finally opened the door, there must have been a line of about twenty people. Boy, if they only knew what was in store. When I finally made it back to my seat, my friend and sister asked me what took so long. I asked how in the heck they figure out that bathroom so quickly and got back to our seats before I did. They both replied, "Well, Sandie, while you were holding us all up, Penny and I went to another bathroom where no one was in line.

Our flight was about five hours which I feel half was spent in the restroom. As we were getting ready to land on the Big Island of Oahu, I peered out the window and I could see Honolulu. The water was a turquoise blue and you could see parts of the coral reef; it was beautiful! Stepping off the plane in Honolulu took your breath away; literally, it took your breath away it was so humid. After we caught our breath, we could appreciate the Hawaiian girls in grass skirts passing out leis. But you do not get them for free, like you see on TV. No, you had to pay something for them. Us girls bought a beautiful lei each because that was a part of coming to Hawaii.

We had to quickly get our luggage to catch another plane to Maui, but it turned out we had an hour delay because the plane going to Maui had to be worked on. I was extremly nervous on this plane because it was much smaller. I didn't dare to attempt to use the restroom. I did not want to imagine being trapped in that cracker box of a bathroom if the plane went down.

It was a very short flight and we landed in Maui safely. What a beautiful place; it was just like what you saw in the movies. Everything was so tropical. Our group had rental cars waiting. We loaded up our luggage and headed to our condo called the Kahana Reef, it was right on the beach. It was like an apartment. As soon as we unpacked and settled in, my sister, Katie, and I put on our swimsuits and ran right into the ocean. It felt like bath water. You can swim anytime of the morning, afternoon, or night and the water remains the same.

We did a lot of sightseeing with my family and friends on Maui. We piled into the cars and took dirt roads all over the island. We saw so many awesome waterfalls. There were little churches sitting all by themselves around all this majestic scenery, as if they were waiting for lost souls. There were tropical flowers so vibrant in color. What amazed me the most, was the bananas. I had no idea bananas grew upside down until I saw it. After doing a little sightseeing, we had lunch and did a little shopping. We picked up a few souvenirs for some of our friends back home, then Katie and I bought T-shirts that said, "Here today, gone to Maui."

Later that evening, Katie and I had our first experience with Maui night life. We went to this place called the Foxy Lady. It reminded me of the movie, *Saturday Night Fever*. They had two great bands that played all the popular disco songs. Of course, we fell in love with all the band members. Then, out of the blue, we met two guys who were islanders. They were very friendly and asked us to dance. Let me take that back, they weren't just cute but a down right hunk of gorgeous! They were construction workers on the island, so they had awesome workout builds with the dark Hawaiian tans.

Anyway, a not so good thing happened that night. As the night progressed, one of the guys turned out to be not so nice. I believe he had too much to drink and he could not handle his liquor. He was not very kind to Katie. My date with Renee, the other one, went very smooth. When Katie and I left, we were so lit, but, hey, we didn't have to pay for any of our drinks so why not get a little lit. Ok, maybe we were a whole lot lit. I truly do not remember how we even made it back to our condo. I know we drove extremely, slow. We were only about fifteen to twenty minutes away from our place, but I think it took us an hour to get there. When we finally arrived, we parked.

As we slowly stepped out of the car and tried to walk normal, I noticed we were at the wrong place. As I was focusing on where we were, I noticed that our condo was across the street. I then mentioned to Katie that we had to cross the street, because we were in the wrong parking lot. As we were crossing, we saw headlights coming our way. Katie and I thought it might be those guys from the Foxy Lady hunting us down, so we tried to run as fast as we could. I am sure we both looked like we were running in slow motion; we had no real feeling in our legs. I bet we both were a sight.

The condo complex had a hedge that lined the street, but there was a hole in the middle of it. We both thought we could run right through that big hole as it appeared to be plenty large enough for us to go through. As we approached and leaped into it, well we quickly discovered it wasn't as big as it appeared. We got stuck in it and our hair tangled in the branches. It's amazing how things appear to be, when you have had just a little too much to drink. The car passed us, and it took some doing but we finally untangled our mess and made our way into the condo.

We tried to be as quite as we could because I sure didn't want to wake my mom or dad. We knew if we did, we'd be in big trouble since we had to get up early to have breakfast and do some sightseeing with the group. Honestly, I do not know how we managed that morning having gone to bed at around 2:00 a.m. and then being forced to wake up at 6:00 a.m. Katie and I had such hangovers. We wanted to stay behind and sleep it off, but my folks wouldn't let us. I remember Mom saying, "We spent a lot of money for this trip, and so did Katie's folks. You are not going partying all night and then sleep all day. You are going to take this trip back home with you so you can share a memory of something great. And not just drinking and partying."

Off we went to breakfast with the rest of the gang and it was the first time any of us tried poi. It looked like chocolate pudding, we all thought it was going to be really good. Once I dipped my fruit into it and it hit my tongue, it felt like slime and I thought I was going to be sick. It tasted like dirt. It was awful, and not because Katie and I were hung over. Everyone else thought the same thing as well.

Sightseeing continued after we ate. Maui is a very beautiful place as I said earlier. Katie and I were sick from partying the night before; I really didn't think we were going to make it through the day. But as the day progressed, our toxic party bodies started to come alive. Heading back to our condo from our very exhausting day, my dad asked if we were going out parting that night. You could hear a real loud "NO!" as Katie and I harmonized together. Instead we hung out by the pool and soaked up that Hawaiian sun to take back awesome Hawaiian tans to show off.

It was overcast as we were lying there, and we both fell asleep. When we woke up, we went in and got cleaned up for dinner. As the night progressed, Katie and I turned red and felt burnt. We were as red as volcano lava and our skin burned like it too. A huge blister formed right in the middle of my chest where there was an open hole on my swimsuit. We couldn't figure out how we got so burnt because it had been so overcast. Someone then told us that overcast weather was worse, and by the looks of us, I guess it was. We were told to sit in the ocean so the saltwater would help and bathe afterward in vinegar water.

While sitting in the ocean, a whole group of stingrays flew up out of the water. You could see them for miles. It was quiet fascinating. Soon my mom called us so each of us could sit in the tub of vinegar for about twenty minutes. It did provide some relief for a short time. After soaking in the ocean and bathing in vinegar, we took a long shower to get the vinegar smell off. The only problem was, even though we showered, I think that vinegar absorbed inside our bodies and the smell was coming out though our pores. Yep, now we knew what my folks' plan was. That was their way from keeping us from going out and partying since no one would want to dance with you if you smelled and looked like a bottle of ketchup.

Before we left Maui, Renee stopped by our condo and asked my folks if he could take me out one last time before we left. He told my dad and mom that he really liked me and wanted to marry me. You should have seen the look on their faces. My mom was the first to speak up, and with her strong German stance, she replied, "Absolutely not. Going out one last time, yes, but marriage, NO! And we had to catch the plane to Oahu in the morning at 9:00 a.m. so she will need to be back at a decent time. Before 11:00 p.m. If you both want to stay in touch, then I suggest exchanging addresses."

So off Renee and I went to the Foxy Lady one last time. As Renee went up to order us a drink, my purse fell off the table. Now mind you, these were those little cocktail tables with those sharp corner edges that were bolted to the floor. As I leaned over to grab my purse and then rose up, my right breast hit the corner of the table. It felt like someone had taken a sledgehammer to it. As the night progressed, it became really swollen and hurt like a son of gun.

When Renee dropped me off, we said our goodbyes and exchanged addresses, then we gave each other the famous Hawaiian hang loose sign. That night I had a really hard time sleeping because the right side of my chest was uncomfortable. It was so swollen and completely black and blue. My poor mom was beside herself. My poor breast looked like some sort of weird experimentation.

When we arrived in Oahu, we all stayed on the tenth floor of the Pink Palace Hotel, which was about a block from the beach. You could see Diamond Head and look down at the beautiful, clear, turquoise blue ocean and white sandy beaches. Katie and I could scope out all those gorgeous tanned surfers from right there.

Every day, I walked up and down those fifteen flights of stairs. Riding fifteen floors in an elevator was just too much for me; I was too claustrophobic. By the end of that vacation, I bet I was the most toned specimen ever. Being young, it really did not bother me to climb those stairs, but I will admit I had to stop and take breaks every so often.

We had four days left before we had to head back to the mainland. We took a glass bottom boat ride, and it was so awesome to see the ocean life under your feet. We went to the beach in the evening to sit and enjoy the surf. One night, we went to a luau and really enjoyed the Hawaiian dancing and the islanders who danced with these long sticks lit on fire. Of course, every restaurant you went in, you would hear the famous Don Ho music playing. You would always hear his most popular song, *Tiny Bubbles*. We always joined in and sang along.

Oahu offered a lot of sightseeing. At the Polynesian Culture Center, Katie and I had our picture taken on a bamboo bridge with palms behind us. We also were not going to go back home without a pucca shell necklace or bracelet as well as a beautiful lei. The day before we left, we took a boat to the Pearl Harbor Memorial where a tour guide told us the heartbreaking story of the sneak attack on our military. On the wall behind where the tour guide stood were all the names of those who lost their lives, and underneath us was the remains of the U.S.S. *Arizona*. The water is so clear you could see the ship covered with sea moss.

On our way back to the shore, dolphins jumped out of the water alongside the boat. They were so close you, you could almost reach out and touch them. I wanted so badly to jump in and swim with them. I still have the desire to swim with them one day.

Katie, my sister, and I had so much to share when we returned to the mainland with our family and the rest of our friends. By this time, my disfigured, burnt, and bruised body was returning to normal, but my mom said I still had to get checked by the doctor. Renee and I wrote each other often, then after a while we lost contact. I will always cherish the time spent in Hawaii and the adventures I had. Someday, I would like to go back to the islands. Who knows, maybe Renee and I might just hook up one day, or maybe I just might get to swim with the dolphins.

Chapter 15

College Challenges

After returning home from Hawaii, it was my time for a big change, moving to Washington state to attend college! My family and I packed up my belongings and headed to the Pacific Northwest. I was very excited on this new adventure, but also nervous on being away from my family and friends.

Leaving town, we looked like the Beverly Hillbillies with the back of my dad's truck piled high with streams of rope going every which way and the back seat of my Love Bug piled high with clothing, shoes, and all my facial care. I think I had more face care, body care, and makeup than anything else combined. We drove into Biggs, Oregon, then crossed the Columbia River, and finally were greeted by the Welcome to Washington sign. Our trip ended at my grandparent's house and all my dad's family were there.

I was so excited to look for an apartment and register for college. Mom and I headed down to the community college campus to sign me up and to buy what books I needed. It was an all-day chore. Since I was not a resident of Washington state, the cost was more, and it entailed more paperwork.

I applied for some part-time jobs that would not interfere with my college schooling. Shortly thereafter, my cousin Brandon told me his mom lived a few houses down from this new duplex and one of them was available. The location was great for me because it was within walking distance to the college. Off my folks and I went to look at this duplex, and it was perfect. It was a one bedroom with a reasonable rent that included water and garbage. Of course $175.00 was a fair price, but working only part-time and making $2.50 an hour, it was quite a big chunk of change for me. Yet, living close to the college was beneficial.

After I was settled in my new place and situated with school, it was time for our goodbyes. My folks needed to head back to California. We all gathered at my grandparent's for dinner. All my aunts, uncles, and cousins reassured my folks that they didn't have to worry about a thing; I would be well-taken care of, which none of us had any doubt. I also had my Aunt Donna and Aunt Emma from my mom's side of the family to stay in contact with. If I got lonely and started missing home, I had plenty of family to keep in touch with. I reassured my folks that I was going to be just fine and that I would see them on their next trip up to Washington. The next day, as my folks and my sis were getting ready to leave, my parents asked one last time if I was sure if this was what I really wanted. I reassured them, this was truly a great fresh start for my own independence and change.

As they drove off, they stopped half-way down the street like they were waiting to see if I would motion for them to come back. My Uncle Lee said, "Well, it looks like Jake and Bonnie are the ones who are going to be lost without Sandie." Pretty soon they just drove on. I know they were having second thoughts about going home without me, and to tell the truth, so was I. When my folks arrived in Biggs, they called my grandparents to check on me one last time to see if I had changed my mind before they drove any further. My grandmother told them everything was good, and to call when they arrived home.

I had another month before school began, so I started working at a drug store taking all the full-time hours I could to make extra money. I knew as soon as school started it was going to be a lot more studying and a lot less working. Money was going to be tight.

One day after work, I stopped by my grandparent's, to check on them. My cousin Brandon was there, and he asked if we could talk privately. Brandon and I were close. We were more like brother and sister than cousins. He asked if he could stay with me awhile. When I asked why, he explained he wasn't getting along with his mom, and that he was seeing a girl he liked very much. He did not want his brothers or dad to know about it because they would embarrass him and her. He felt she wouldn't want anything to do with him then. At this time, Brandon's mom and dad were divorced. He knew how to pull at my heart strings, and it worked every time. I told him he could move in with me, but there would be no parties or other people in and out. Most of all, he was to stay in school, or I would be angry. He knew I meant it. He brought a cot over to my place and set it up on the far side of the living room.

Brandon had a real hang up with his hair, actually, he had a really nice head of hair, thick and wavy; it was every girl's dream hair. But when it came to his, he was worse than a woman about the way it looked; it had to be just right. He would spend hours fixing it. You could hear him sometimes in the bathroom, saying things like, "Oh come on, work for me today," or other times you would hear more choice words as the hair spray would go off. One day, he came dancing out of the bathroom with his new John Travolta hair style, like in the movie, *Staying Alive*. "Well, what do you think, cuz?" I told him it looked nice, but, with the amount of hair spray he used, he'd better hope no bugs landed in it because they would be there for a while. He was one of Aqua Net's best customers. We both laughed at that comment.

Before Brandon was on his way out the door to see the love of his life, I asked if he could start the dishwasher. I went to get ready for work, listening to the radio and singing along. I then heard this weird sound. As I turned the radio down to clearly hear it, I peered out the bedroom door and could not believe what I saw. There coming out of the kitchen into the hall by the front door was this huge mass of bubbles. It looked like something from a horror movie. I screamed and ran to the kitchen and noticed it was coming from the dishwasher. I quickly turned it off. I looked on the counter and noticed Brandon had added dish soap instead of dishwasher soap. I guess that's what happens when you are so in love, you don't even realize what you are doing.

I called Katie and spoke with Brandon. I proceeded to let him know all that hair spray and being in love made him a real bird head and he wasn't aware of what he is doing. He asked me what I was talking about, I told him he added the wrong soap to the dishwasher and now I had a whole kitchen and hallway covered in bubbles. He informed me that Katie and him, would be over to clean up the mess. I thanked him and told him to please pay attention next time.

After I hung up the phone, I realized I might have hurt his feelings with what I just said and how I just sounded. He probably was thinking I sounded just like his mother. Before I headed out the door, I left him a note explaining I was sorry for what I had said and to have a great rest of his day. When I returned home that afternoon from work, I was convinced I was going to walk into a mess because Brandon probably forgot to come by since he was in love and afraid to mess his hair up.

When I opened the door and walked in, I was amazed at how great everything looked. On the counter was a note from Brandon that read, "Thank u cuz for all you do for me, and I am really sorry for not paying more attention when I added the dish soap. Honestly, I did not think it would make that big of a mess. And guess what! My hair stayed in place the whole time while cleaning up the mess. You were right about things sticking to my hair though, all the bubbles stuck to it. I looked like a giant cotton ball. I will see you later this evening. Love, your favorite cuz!" After I read his humorous note, I felt bad on how I had spoken to him earlier.

When Brandon walked in later that evening, he gave me that look he always did, pulling at my heart. I told him I was truly sorry for getting upset the way I did. He smiled and said it was ok because he should have been paying more attention. I then asked, "By the way, how much of that dish soap did you use?" He told me he had filled both cups. No wonder we had such bubble blob.

I had about two weeks left till school started. One day, while visiting with my grandparents, my cousins Karen and Jeremy were there and needed a ride home. I had to take Washington Ave. which had a speed limit of 55 mph. The city had just opened a new road, off of Washington Ave., this being 40th Ave.

So here we were heading down Washington Ave. with my Love Bug doing 55 mph, Jeremy in the front seat and Karen in the back. As we turned down 40th Ave, I picked up speed back to 55 mph. Out of nowhere, these flashing lights went off behind me. I had never been pulled over before, I was so nervous.

Jeremy told me to pull over while Karen was in the back laughing. Everything was funny to her. I pulled over, of course, I started crying. Jeremy handed me my registration from the glove box and told me to get my license out and to quit crying because the cop was not going to feel sorry for me. I was so upset with the whole ordeal that I yelled at Karen to hush up!

About that time, the officer was at my window. He asked me why I was speeding, I told him I truly did not realize I was doing so. He informed me there was a speed limit sign that said 40 mph and I was going 55 mph. That was grounds for a ticket. He also asked why I was crying, of course, Karen started in with her laughing again. At this point I have heard enough of her constant laugh. I really got angry with her, shook my fist, and told her to shut the blanketly-blank up. She then shut up, and Jeremy proceeded to tell the officer I was nervous and had just moved here.

The officer asked to see my registration, license, and insurance. I was handing it to him when I suddenly remembered watching a TV program about police always picking on out-of-staters. I still had my Cali license plates. Then, something stirred up inside me and this boldness came into my voice as I said, "The real reason you pulled me over was because of my out-of-state license plates, and I heard on TV that cops are always picking on out-of-staters." He informed me that wasn't the reason, but he did mention that if I thought this was why he pulled me over, then he would just add a little extra onto my ticket. He calmly handed me a $75.00 ticket with a grin, told me to have a great day, and make sure I watched my speed.

I cried like a baby. How was I ever going to pay this? Jeremy couldn't understand why the officer hadn't give me a warning. He then told Karen she, better not say a word to her mom or anyone for that matter We knew she had a big mouth, and news would spread like fire. Karen said she wouldn't, but Jeremy and I knew better. I dropped Karen off at home, then took Jeremy home, and finally headed back to my little corner of the world.

When I returned home, Brandon was there with Katie. After visiting with them, I started to calm down some. Later Jeremy called. He was checking to see if I was doing ok and if Aunt Gina had called yet. I informed him I was doing much better and I hadn't heard from her, as of yet, but I was sure she would be calling soon. The next day, sure enough, the phone rang, and Aunt Gina asked if I wanted to come over for dinner. I knew exactly why I was invited. I thought, "What the heck. I can't hide from it forever." Besides my aunt worked at the courthouse so she would find out sooner or later. Just maybe I could have my ticket deferred since it was my first one.

Pulling up in front of my aunt's house, I dreaded going in because I knew my getting a ticket was going to be made into big deal. When we sat down to dinner, the first words I heard was my aunt mentioning how I could go in front of the judge and let him know that I was going to college and only working part-time. She thought he would more than likely give me a big break, or give me a deferment since it was my first one. When Monday rolled around, I called the courthouse to set up a date to get my very first ticket taken care of.

I parked my Love Bug in the north parking lot when the day came and entered the courthouse. I asked the front desk clerks if they could direct me to where I was supposed to go for a speeding ticket. I was told to go to the second floor and someone there would direct me to the right court room. As I entered, I sat down in the third row from the door, right next to the aisle. A voice said, "All rise for honorable judge so-and-so." The judge then called his first case, the second, then the third. I noticed everyone who was going before him was being sentenced for hard crimes, like a drug bust and shop lifting; there were even a few in orange suits with shackles. I knew then I was in the wrong court room.

Standing next to me was an officer, so I lightly tapped his arm and proceeded to tell him, I think I'm in the wrong court room. He then asked, what was I there for, I then mentioned, I was there only for a speeding ticket. He looked at me with a grin and said I was in the right place. Just about the time he said that, the judge called my name. My heart was pounding so hard and I was shaking as I approached where my appointed attorney stood. I was scared to death and could feel everyone's eyes all on me. The judge sternly asked me to move up to the bench next to my geeky attorney who was wearing those big old, black, birth control glasses. I'm thinking to myself, "How in the heck is this dorky looking character going to speak for me?"

My attorney proceeded to explain my case to the judge using all his legal terminology. He further added that I was not familiar with the area having just moved here from California, and that I was only working part-time and attending college. He then did his attorney duty and commented to the judge, that Ms. Hann would appreciate if, your Honor would be so gracious as to lessen the ticket amount or allow a deferment since it was Ms. Hamm's first ticket.

I did think it went over well with the judge. I thought to myself wouldn't it have been easier just say I had been speeding and to finish it off with the fact I was going to school rather than give my whole life story. As I stood there looking at the judge, he put his head down and looked at me through the top of his glasses. With a deep, stern voice he said, "Ms. Hann, how do you plea?" He scared me so bad, and, from what I had heard with all the other sentencing before me, I immediately broke down crying and begging him to please, please not put me in jail. I promise I will never speed again.

The whole court room laughed, and the judge even snickered. I whipped around facing everyone else waiting their turn to come fourth and blurted out, "I don't' know what is so funny, but I am sure you won't be laughing when you have to come before the judge."

The judge hit his gavel on his desk and instructed for order in the court. There was silence, except for my crying. The judge then had my attorney approach the bench with my ticket so he could reduce the amount. He then told me to stop by the window in the hall outside the court room to set up a date to pay it. I was never so happy to walk out of that court room.

As I made my way to the exit, everyone stared at me and some even smiled. As I was about to leap out the door, the judge called to me one last time. "Ms. Hann." I turned around shaking with tears rolling down my cheeks again. He informed me he never had a performance like that ever in his career as a judge and wanted to thank me for giving him a good laugh. I felt so humiliated, then thought to myself, he meant what he said or he was being sarcastic.

Whichever it was, I was so relieved to walk out of those courtroom doors. As I approached the window to set up a date to pay my ticket, I looked down and saw the judge who liked my sense of humor apparently had no heart. He had reduced my ticket a lousy ten bucks. I had gone through all that in that ungodly, forsaken courtroom for a lousy $10.00? Boy, was my Aunt Gina going to hear about this one.

As I left the courthouse, walking towards the parking lot, I noticed a police officer was standing by my car, looking at my license plates, and writing me up. I ran toward him yelling and crying again. "Please, please, officer! I just came from paying a ticket after being stuck in a court room with criminals, a geeky attorney, a not-so-caring judge, and a room full of laughing fools. Please officer, give me a break." He took pity on me and told me he would cut me some slack. He then told me to look around and notice where I had parked. He asked, "Did you not see and read the sign as you entered?"

I looked up around me and saw I was parked in a police zone. Boy, did I ever feel stupid. I learned a real valuable lesson that day, first, not to ever get in trouble with the law, and have to go through a horrific courtroom trial, and second, to always read signs and pay attention to where you are.

At this time, I still was not a walking Christian. Driving to my grandparents, my mind wondered back to my Christian friends, Lisa and Maria, and how they would tell me when things were in disorder in a person's life, it was the enemy coming up against them. I really don't know why, but I had such an interest in finding out more about God and Jesus, and how I could have the same relationship as Lisa, Marie, and my Aunt Glenda and Uncle Al. They all told me how I could get there, but it had to be felt. I was told someday God would convict my heart and I would get there in His timing.

Upon arriving at my grandparents, I told them all what had transpired on my day in court. They all thought my story was hilarious.

School was ready to start, so I put the whole ticket ordeal behind me. The first day was great. I had some cool teachers and met a few other students who were also from out of state. As I walked home that day, I thought to myself, "This is going to be a great and fresh start for me."

However, as time went on with school and work, I felt the pressure build, plus I was doing terrible on my tests. I did fine in class, but when the tests came around, I did not do so well. I had test anxiety so bad just like I did in high school. I had an appointment with a school counselor who told me I had to get my test scores up or I would have to drop out. I was so discouraged at this point. I went home that day and just bawled till there was nothing left to come out of my tear ducts. I knew my family was going to be upset with me and think I wasn't studying enough or was too busy doing other things.

Before I called my folks, I called my Aunt Glenda. I told her what was happening with my schooling and she was so understanding. I told her I recognized Mom and Dad paid a lot for me to go to college and had helped me move up here. "They both are going to be so unhappy and disappointed in me." She then said something so reassuring to me it was like an angel was right there with me. She said, "Sometimes in life we all make hurry-up decisions without really thinking them through, and a lot of us don't go to God and really listen to what He tells our hearts because we always listen to what others say or think for us."

I connected what my aunt said to what I heard before from Lisa and Maria. Aunt Glenda mentioned that maybe I need a break for a semester and then take some classes at the college that could help me with different studying strategies. As we said our goodbyes and love you, I felt so much better. I was going to go to the college tomorrow and take a different approach.

At this time, Christmas break was approaching, I had passed first semester, but I knew when school started up after the New Year, I would have to take some extra-help study classes. Upon returning to school, I studied hard and believed the extra study classes would help me get through my next semester. Towards the end of the school year, before summer break, we had finals. I went into a freeze mode again with test anxiety once more. I felt like such a failure. I did not pass any of my finals.

I headed home in tears and called my folks to let them know I was ready to move back home. I had enough of Yakima and enough of school. My dad made the statement, "Well, Sandie, sometimes things just don't work out like we plan." That was a very unusual statement coming from my dad because it was something, ordinarily he wouldn't say. I started packing things up in boxes, so it would be less to do, when my parents came to get me, we could just load up and go. The rest of the Washington family didn't want me to leave, but I felt like this wasn't where I was supposed to be. I took all my books back to the college, signed my release papers, and walked away with many mixed emotions.

A couple of weeks later, my dad arrived with my friend Kari whom I had had the falling out with before I left California because of the situation with Mark. I had a last few days to spend with my cousins, cruising the Ave., swimming, and seeing movies. When it came time for me to head back home, I said my last goodbyes. There were many swollen eyes from crying, but we knew we would be seeing each other again, just like in the past.

Before we left Yakima, we had to stop and fuel up. I told my dad that some adventures were just not meant to be. As we headed out of Yakima, it occurred to me I was trying to mimic other people going to college after graduating high school. I felt like I had to accomplish a degree and make all my family proud of me. But I guess that was not in God's plan at the time. I remembered what my Aunt Glenda told me; she said God made us all unique, He fashioned us specifically for His call in our lives and not for someone else's, and to allow Him to show me my unique qualities as the world didn't need more copies. Recalling that, I feel at peace with myself and all was well.

Chapter 16

My Life
After College

As we left Washington state and headed back to California, I could not help but sing that song "California here I come, right back where I started from." I thought of what I had left behind for those couple of years in Yakima and what I was going back to. It was a good time for Kari and I to seek forgiveness with each other on what had happened with Mark. We both shed a lot of tears, but we knew this was the beginning of our healing, as we moved on to reminiscing about all the things that took place at Intel. Kari still worked there and mentioned our drill sergeant, old Serpentine Fire, as I had called her, had left and they had a new drill sergeant who was not quite as bad. We laughed and talked about the old times in high school and our old stomping grounds. We had a lot to catch up on, we seemed to cover it all the whole way back to Cali.

Arriving on our street, I noticed Tommy, my dear friend and the boy next door, standing by his car. As we drove past, he waved, and a big smile came over his face. He looked like a kid with his face pressed up against a candy shop window. I noticed some changes in our neighborhood as we pulled into the driveway. It is funny just in the space of a year or two, there can be so many changes. Yes, being back home was where I needed to be.

As Kari drove off, Tom came down the street to chat. He mentioned he was home on leave. It was so nice to see him; he always had such a special place in my heart. He was always respectful and honest, not only to me but to my family as well. We came from two different lifestyles. He came from a family of partiers who had a lot of family fights, drinking, and so on. My family was a very reserved middle-class family. So, some of my family was not too fond of him and some of his family was not too fond of me. But whatever the case, we had a strong friendship bond, and, to us, it did not matter what others thought.

I started looking for a job and tried to decide what I was going to do with my life. I thought about maybe going back to college, thinking now that I was back home things might be different. I talked it over with my folks and they both said to do whatever I wanted to do, but to make sure and really think things through.

As I listened to what my folks had said, my thoughts wondered back to my high school years and my two Christian friends, Lisa and Marie. They always told me to pray and ask God for guidance in situations like these, so that's what I did. I always used the basement as my place to have a one-on-one talk with Jesus. The only thing is, sometimes I felt like He wasn't listening to me. I thought it was because I didn't have a relationship with Him like Lisa, Maria, and my aunt and uncle had. I did know who He was, but obviously there was more to it. I had hoped that one day I would share the same experience as other walking Christians. But then, I wasn't sure if I was ready. Maybe God was not ready for me, so I thought.

That following Friday, Tommy came over and asked if I wanted to take a drive down to Monterey and help him look for an apartment since he was going to be stationed at Fort Ord. I did not hesitate to reply that I would love to go. The problem was convincing my folks to allow me. Tom asked my parents, and they both were kind of hesitant at first. It took them awhile to respond, but after they had thought about it, they came to an agreement saying yes. Tommy said he was leaving around 7:00 in the morning. I told him I would be ready.

Monterey is such a beautiful costal town, right next door to Carmel, and home to a lot of celebrities. It was very serene four hour drive down the coast. Tommy had always thought my family was rich, which we weren't, but he thought so when he compared his family to mine. His family had so much chaos and there was always fighting. That was the major reason why he enlisted in the military, so he could get out of the rut he was in and better himself. I remember him saying how he had wanted to enlist in the Air Force, and that he tried a couple of times, but just couldn't get his test score high enough, so the Army is where he ended up. Boy, could I ever relate to the test score thing.

As soon as we hit Monterey, we started looking for an apartment. We really didn't have to look too hard or all day. Marina was a small military town next to the base just outside of Monterey. We were happy to learn a new apartment complex had just opened, so we went to check it out. Tom was in luck! There was one apartment left and the rent was affordable. After he put down his deposit and signed all the paperwork, we decided to drive around There is nothing more soothing and tranquil than the beach and ocean. What a beautiful place!

I told Tom I would drive down some weekends and visit him. He really liked that idea because he knew his family wouldn't come; he'd have to drive up to see them. After a month or so, one Friday night, I received a phone call from Tom. He had come home for the weekend and was staying at his sister's house in Union City. He asked if I wanted to go to dinner later that evening with both his sisters and brothers-in-law. He said he'd pick me up around 4:30 pm.

Tommy took me to one of the best Mexican restaurants in town. As we were sitting around the table after the waitress had taken our order, I noticed Tommy giving his brother-in-law, Jack, the eye. It seemed like they were passing something around to each other under the table. When it reached Tommy, he slowly put this little black velvet box on the table in front of me. When I opened it, there was the most beautiful diamond, heart-shaped ring. I asked, what was the occasion as his sisters kept saying, "Come on, Tommy, hurry up with it." Finally, he asked if I would marry him. I was at first in awe at the ring in front of me. What a lot to take in!

There was so much to think about. First, Tommy needed to approach my folks, and we both knew that wasn't going to be an easy task. While we were all sitting there eating our dinner and discussing how Tom was going to approach my parents, I suggested I should feel them out first and show them the ring. After that, I felt Tommy could come over and have a heart-to-heart talk with them. When I got home that evening, my folks asked me how my night went. I told them it was great! Then I showed them the ring. It was exactly as I expected. They did not know Tom like I did. They had only seen the family he grew up in, so I guess in their eyes that was the life they thought I was going to live.

After they made their comments, I came back with a stern angry voice. "That is how you have always been. You look at one side and make your judgment of someone. Just like you do with me. You never give anyone a chance." Then I really went off and told them they had always judged me on every-thing and would always listen to someone else's opinion instead of thinking it through and looking at all angles.

I could not believe I had talked to my folks that way and stood up for myself. I could see the fire escalating in my mother's eyes and her German blood boiling. I turned and walked into my room while she was still in a rage. I thought for sure she was going to enter my room at any moment and put me in a coma. Then everything went quiet. I just sat on my bed crying and staring at this beautiful, heart-shaped diamond ring in this black velvet box from someone who really cared for me. I cried myself to sleep.

Tom came over the next morning. My folks hadn't said too much to me that morning and I hadn't either. When I invited him to come in, I could tell he was nervous. I am sure he felt the tension. As he sat down in the living room and we both were talking, my folks joined us. They asked a million ques-tions. Tommy's response was very sincere and respectful. I guess we both were in the clear for the time being.

We sat our wedding date for July. I was twenty-two at the time. We invited only immediate family. We were married in the Little Brown Church of Sunol, which is a quaint, little, wine town nestled back in the hills not far from my home-town. We had our wedding reception in the back yard of my parents' home, and all went well. My folks' 25th anniversary was just a few days after our wedding day. During our recep-tion, some anniversary gifts were exchanged as well as wed-ding gifts. My aunt and uncle from Los Angeles came up as a surprise for my folks' anniversary. My mom's cousin Janis and her husband Tony stopped by for a short time. When the day ended, Tom and I said our goodbyes and headed back to Monterey.

We planned our honeymoon for Washington state so Tom could meet more of my relatives. Before we left, my mom called stating Janis and Tony had been in a car accident after leaving our reception. Janis had messed up her arm bad, but they were both doing ok. I felt guilty that Janis and Tony had been in an accident. You see, I had kept our wedding to just immediate family only for cost reasons and to prevent a family feud with who was invited and who was not. Keeping it simple seemed the way to go. I felt guilty because if I had invited them, they might have stayed longer, and the accident might not have occured. Janis is also my godmother, which made the guilt even stronger. I told Mom to give Janis and Tony my love, and I would catch up with them when I got back from Washington.

We had a great drive and great time in Washington, and an awesome visit with family. Tom really enjoyed his time and seemed to get along with everyone just fine. We were there for about a week, and the day we left, we stopped by one more time to visit my grandmother who was in a nursing home and not doing well. She had a big smile on her face When we walked in, grandma again asked who this young man was. He replied, "Tom. Do you remember me from the other day when we were discussing how you knew my grandmother and grandfather in Arkansas?" She asked if she was right in thinking that was Fannie Bell and Shelby. It is amazing how, when we reach that certain age, we can forget the present but remember the past.

As we kissed her on the cheek and said our goodbyes, I told Grandma I would stay in touch by writing. She told me not to forget; I told her I wouldn't. I did write her when we got back to Monterey, and when I spoke to my Aunt Gina, she said Grandma had received the letter and still remembered Tom's grandparents whom I had mentioned in the letter. I continued to send her cute thinking of you cards with a letter attached. After a few months, I received the sad news from my folks that my grandmother had passed. Tom could not take any leave time, so I went with my folks up to Washington to my grandmother's funeral. What a sad day. The family shared a lot of memories about what Grandma use to do and say. We would all laugh, then cry. Yes, loved ones may pass, but their memory is always in our hearts.

Tommy and I made a lot of friends while we were stationed in Fort Ord. I worked part-time at a doughnut shop there in Marina just a few blocks from where we lived. There I learned how to make doughnuts, and I also made lunches. I enjoyed the work plus it kept me busy while Tom worked long hours on base or continued his training or played war. It is really a different life being married to a GI.

I will never forget, one particular day spent in ER at Silas B. Hayes Hospital on base. I was running a temperature of 102, could not swallow, was achy all over, and both of my ears were killing me. As I sat in the hall waiting to see a doctor, the MPs brought this poor, battered woman who had been beaten terribly. Her face was swollen and a mass of bruises. She was crying as the MPs told her she needed to press charges. I remember her saying how she was afraid that he would come after her if she did. They reassured her that once the charges were filed, they would serve him, and his unit would be made aware; he would be arrested.

I finally got fed up with her disputing everything they were telling her. I stood up and walked over to her and told her if she did not press charges then she deserved getting beat up. And furthermore, I would take the same broom stick he beat her with and do the same job to him. The MPs just stood there while I tried to talk some sense into her. I was not feeling well and was tired of waiting and listening to her accepting this beating like she was meant to receive it. The MP officers tried to calm the situation, especially with me.

Finally, I heard a nurse call me back to an examination room. When the doctor came in, he told me I caused quite a little scene out in the waiting room, and that whatever I said to that poor young women sunk in because she finally accepted pressing charges. I felt such relief for her, and now I was getting some medical relief as well. It was as I expected; I had strep throat and infections in both ears. As I left the hospital with my prescription of penicillin, I saw that poor battered women sitting in the MP vehicle. My heart ached for her because her soul was so broken and had been for such a long time with this man who was supposed love her and respect her. I also felt relief for her, just knowing she was going to be ok. I hoped the next man who came into her life would give her the love and respect she deserved.

Chapter 17

My New Life as a Military Wife

The first couple of months in my new life as a military wife weren't too bad. I made new friendships, worked part-time at a doughnut shop, and hopefully made a difference in a battered woman's life. After being on my meds for a week following my strep throat and ear infections, I went back to work making doughnuts. Once in awhile, I would bring doughnuts home after work for the neighbors and other friends. I always put little notes on them that said, "Made by Sandie from the kitchen of Don's Doughnuts." I have to admit, I made some pretty awesome doughnuts. Even my boss agreed.

After a few weeks went by, I started getting sick and didn't feel right. I told my friend Carol that I was getting sick to my stomach at work and when I smelled those doughnuts, I'd break out into a sweat. A big smile came over her face and she said, "Sandie, I think you are going to be a mom." I had that suspicion but really did not want to be a mother at that time because Tom and I had only been married for a few months. We knew there would be family things said because of us just starting out. Here was another step in my life that my folks were not going to be happy about. They were not excited about me marrying Tom, and they sure arn't going to be excited about having a grandchild either.

Carol reassured me everything was going to work out and first things first. I needed to go to the doctor and find out for sure. She went with me to the clinic on base where they ran some tests. After Carol and I left, we had lunch and talked about our lives and our families. Our husbands were out for a few days on maneuvers, so it was a good time to regroup myself, find out if I was pregnant, and take it from there.

The next day I went back to the clinic with Carol and the doctor told me that the pregnancy test had come back positive. I was in total shock and started crying. I asked the doctor, "How could this happen?" He and Carol started laughing, and the doctor said, "Did you not learn about the birds and the bees?" Then Carol continued with, "And the flowers and the trees." As I sat there in disbelief, I realized what I had said had not come out right. "No, that's not what I meant," I explained "I have been on birth control, so how could this have happened?"

The doctor asked me a few questions, like had I been sick lately and been on medication. I told him I had been on anti-biotics for about fourteen days for strep and ear infections. He then explained that some antibiotics can encourage the break-down and decrease of estrogen in the body which can lower the effectiveness of birth control pills. As I listened and took all this in, I was and wasn't relieved. I scheduled my first OB appointment and left the clinic full of mixed feelings.

Carol told me to relax and that everything would work its way out. The news was not going to go well with my family and Tom's. But, first priority was breaking the news to Tom. Neither of us had wanted to start a family so soon, I was unsure of what Toms reaction would be. Carol and I planned a couples dinner, when Tom returned from his maneuvers so I could tell him with some help from Carol. I thought it would be a little easier with good friends around.

The big night came, and I was very surprised by Tom's reply and action. He was very surprised, but not too upset. It wasn't as bad as I thought it would be. It was also easier with a little help from our friends. Now the next big step was telling our folks. That defiantly was going to be a real challenge on both our parts. Tom and I discussed how we were going to break the news to our families. I was a total wreck on how I was going to approach my folks.

We decided to visit our families for the weekend after a couple of weeks had gone by. We stopped by Tom's sister's house first in Union City and told her and her husband the news. They didn't say much at first, but then they started in on a baby is a big responsibility, which did not sit well with either of us because of issues I will not mention. After about an hour into our visit, as we were leaving, his sister said best of luck with the news and telling the rest of the family.

At that moment, I just wanted to go back home. On our way to Livermore, I said to Tom that if we got any negative feedback from anyone, I would cut our weekend short and head back to Monterey. When we arrived into town, we visited with my folks for a while. Finally, I broke the news that they were going to be grandparents. At first, my mom and dad did not say anything at all. They both just looked at each other. I remember my mom getting up from the couch and walking into the kitchen, and my dad just sitting there staring at the TV focused on what he was watching. I told Tom, "Well, I guess we better go over to your folks." I walked into the kitchen to give my mom a hug and she kind of pulled away, only asking if we were coming back for dinner. I told her I would call and let her know. I gave my dad a hug, and Tom told them both we would see them later.

As we scooted out the door, I said, "I knew this was going to happen." My husband smiled and said, "Don't get to discouraged. We have the rest of my family to break the news to." I answered that I really did not want any more negativity. When we arrived at Tom's folks, his mom was making homemade biscuits for the next morning's breakfast and his dad was watching some western movie. When we sat down in the kitchen, I asked Tom's mom if she needed help with anything and she replied with a forceful "no!" She swung around and looked at both of us with kind of a stern look on her face and asked Tom if he wanted a cup of coffee. His dad walked in and joined us.

As we sat there while Tom and his dad sipped their coffee, Tom's dad unexpectedly questioned, "Are you both sure you will be able to handle a new addition to the family?" Tom and I looked at each other and immediately said, "Boy, news travels fast." Some family just don't know how to keep their mouths shut. His folks already knew I was pregnant before we arrived. Tom's mom joined in saying, "Having a baby is a big responsibility, and you will be gone a lot, Tom. Are you both sure you thought this through?" I thought, "How can everyone be so against us?" At that instant, something came over me and I came back with, "Well, things do happen, just like they did when you both ended up with six children. I am sure your folks said the same thing to you, right?" There was silence. Nothing else was said, other than his mother asking if we wanted to come by in the morning for breakfast before heading back to Monterey.

Time went by. One Saturday, I asked Tom if he would like to take a drive down to Carmel and Monterey for the day. Driving around Monterey, we ran across this cute, little, white house with a white picket fence that had a For Rent sign. We stopped and looked in the windows, and the neighbors came out. We asked them if they knew much about the house and the landlord. They were a very nice couple about our age and had three boys, the youngest was about a year old. The husband worked construction and the wife was a stay-at-home mom. They told us the people who owned the house owned quite a few hotels in Monterey, and very well-known, and very pleasant. Their son used to live in the house. Of course, I'm sure the son lived there for free or for a very small amount of rent.

We thanked them and called the number on the rental sign. Tom spoke to the lady, and she agreed to meet us there to look at the house. It came furnished, except for the kitchen table, which was fine because we had a kitchen table. I fell in love with the house. The rent was reasonable and included water and garbage service. After Tom filled out the application, she said she would call us in the next day or two and let us know if we had the place or not.

When she left, Tom and I discussed the rent, trying to determine how much more it was than what we were paying now. Back home, we put all our monthly bills and rent on paper to see if we could manage a little more in rent money. Our car and some of our small bills had been paid off, so after we looked at our finances, we could swing it. And it would be so nice to live in a house rather than apartment.

When the owner had shown us around the house, she'd mentioned the neighbors next to us were a wonderful

Christian couple. I told her that we had met them when we had stopped to look around. It seemed like God was always putting Christians in my path. I knew that house was where we needed to be. The next day, I received a call from Mrs. Bastanelli telling me the house was ours. I was so ecstatic, I told her I would bring the deposit and rent to her that day. I couldn't let Tom know till that evening because I couldn't call his battalion. I knew he, too, would be excited.

When I drove up to the Bastanelli's home, I was in awe over such a beautiful place. She greeted me at the door and invited me in. There I met her husband, as we sat at the kitchen table chatting like we were old friends. What wonderful people they were. After I handed over the rent and deposit and received the receipt, she handed me the key. I asked if they knew who lived in that huge home on the hill up from us. They both smiled, saying they did know him and were good friends. Mrs. Bastanelli asked if I was familiar with older singers and I said yes, somewhat, from my mom listening to them. She asked if I had ever heard of Paul Anka. I answered yes, sharing that my mother loved his songs and played them often. She then said with a smile, that the huge home was Paul Anka's. I was so excited because here I now lived down the hill from someone famous.

Tom and I had a yard sale to get rid of things we were not going to need since our new home was already furnished. That evening, we had Mike, Carol, and their little one over for dinner. Carol told us they were going to be moving too. When asked where, Mike said he just was put on orders to Germany and they would be leaving in the next month. Carol and their son would stay with her folks until Mike found a place and send for them. We would always stay in touch. After a month had went by, we said our last goodbyes to Mike and Carol, wishing them the best.

During the months in our little house, I began to really show and was constantly sick. I had a horrible time with this pregnancy. Our neighbors were so good with us, and Kathy always made up dishes and brought them over. My mom threw me a baby shower at home in Livermore, and I received so many wonderful baby gifts. That was the first time I saw my mom excited to be a grandma, and the first time I was excited to be a mom. Tommy and I had to cut our stay short because he had to leave very early Monday morning for a week of maneuvers.

That afternoon, as we drove into Monterey, a huge sheet of fog was rolling in. The fog is super thick in Monterey because it is so close to the ocean. We were down to one vehicle, at this time, so the plan was for me to drop Tom off on post at 5:00 a.m. in the dark. Now it looked like it was going to be in this fog. The alarm sounded at 4:00 a.m. I dreaded driving in such thick stuff where one could barely see. I drove slowly, the fog was so thick you couldn't even see the white lines on the road. As I dropped Tom off in front of the battalion and we said our goodbyes, he told me to be careful going back home. When I drove away from the battalion, I was totally turned around on base. It seemed like I was driving for a long time to get to the entrance. I was getting more and more nervous because the fog seemed like it was getting thicker and I could see less and less where I was. I remember driving past this gate with a sign that read "Warning - Restricted Area" in big, bold, red lettering. I knew then I was in deep trouble.

I was looking for a place to turn around when I saw two soldiers coming toward me with their guns drawn. They asked me to pull over to the side of the road. I started crying, not knowing what was going to happen. Here I was with no makeup, in my pajamas and robe, telling them I just dropped my husband off at his unit and was turned around and lost in this stupid fog. They were sympathetic and told me one of them would have me follow him to the front entrance of the base. I was so embarrassed, but also very thankful. I even gave one of the soldiers a huge thank you hug, still sobbing from being so scared but relieved at the same time.

Later that day, I had an ultrasound and it showed we were having a girl. I was getting tired of being pregnant and wanted it to be over. I started to decorate the nursery a little bit and put all the baby clothes in the dresser that my folks had bought us along with a crib as well.

That week Tom was gone, I felt overwhelmed and the week just seemed to drag on. Now, it was only three more days till he would be back home. To help pass the time, I visited with my neighbor, Kathy. We really enjoyed each other's company. She was always busy with her three boys, and she was such a strong woman of faith. Even through her tough times, she was always cheerful and explained to me, God always works things out in His time because His timing is always perfect. We just needed to stay faithful and truly trust Him.

On this particular day visiting with her, I proceeded to tell her I had heard that very same thing from all the people who were faithful Christians who had crossed my path. I knew there was something different about these friends and family who had so much faith. I asked Kathy why did so many people put Christians down.

Kathy continued to explain that what gives Christians a bad name is when a person claims to be one and then lives the opposite way. She likened it to a bad cop who is supposed to uphold the law and is corrupt instead, and to a politician who is supposed to uphold the constitution, freedoms, and liberties but doesn't. Those types of people think they are above the law, she explained further, just like someone who says they are a believer but think they can be above God's law.

My whole being started hurting right then. My eyes got all watery and I felt so horrible about myself because I was one of those people who let the enemy take control. Kathy told me God would work through me in His timing. She encouraged that I would get there, saying, "You have such a big heart for others, and I have seen your actions with certain things. I do believe the Holy Spirit is working in you. Just stay focused on His Word. It is a daily struggle because we live in a sinful world in a sinful body, as long as you stay strong in the Holy Spirit and His Word, He will always be there, and one day your heart will be convicted. Trials are what keeps us from seeking Him." I called my Aunt Glenda after my discussion with Kathy and shared what I had just experienced. I knew she would understand because she and my uncle were so strong in their walk of faith.

After I hung up with my aunt, I switched to thinking about names for our new baby girl. I had spent hours thinking of names. The nurse from my OB appointment that week had told me that, by the looks of my ultrasound, I was going to be due around the end of April. That's when it hit me. I was going to name our baby girl April. I have always loved that name. April was my birthday month, and our daughter was going to be born in April as well. The name was perfect.

Just about then, the phone rang and this voice on the other end said, "Hey, I'm back. You want to come pick me up?" Tom was home! Yes, I had been on overload the whole week he was gone, but what I did know in that moment was that my husband had made it home safely, I finally had a baby named picked, but most of all, I had the experience I felt within my soul when Kathy and her loving grace changed my inner spirit about Jesus's loving grace for me.

Chapter 18

The Birth of
Our Daughter

As the months followed and the more my belly grew, the sicker I became. It was May, and no baby yet. I didn't experience morning sickness; for me, it was all day sickness. I was so miserable.

I told Tom I had another OB appointment and asked if he could go with me. Tom didn't get to go with me very often. He was always gone off playing war or doing whatever soldiers do. He said he would and told his commander I was having issues with my pregnancy. Tom's sergeant wasn't very sympathetic with my pregnancy issues. He made it clear to Tom that if the military had wanted you to have a wife, they would have issued him one. How could someone say something so upsetting and wrong? Well, when it comes to the government, that is their mentality.

At this time, I was so puffy I looked like the Pillsbury Dough Boy, my ankles were Tankles, and my blood pressure was running extremely high. The doctors were keeping a close check on me because I had developed toxemia (now known as preeclampsia). I wanted this whole pregnancy to be over; I was so sick and so done with it. I asked the doctors if they could just induce me and get it over with, but they said no. Sounds like the military, taking control of not only your husband's life but yours as well. Since I had to wait to go into labor naturally, I just sat around all day with my feet elevated and feeling terrible. I did get a chance to talk to Tom about what he thought of the name April, even though it was already the month of May. He wasn't too crazy about it and said we still had time to come up with names.

The next morning when I woke up, I was soaking wet and so was the bed. I cried out for Tom, saying, 'I think my water broke." He jumped up and threw on some sweats, and I jumped in the shower. I remember him telling me not to worry about a shower but to just throw some clothes on and get to the hospital. I was so upset at this time, and I felt like I needed to clean myself. I did a real fast wash, threw on my sweats and sweatshirt, and away we went. The whole way Tom kept asking me if I was having contractions. I told him I wasn't and was worried because I wasn't feeling anything. I kept asking him over and over if he thought everything was going to be ok. He was so nervous his voice was shaky, and I knew he was trying to be calm while reassuring me that everything was going to be just fine. Honestly, I think he was trying to reassure himself.

I was crying and all stressed out which stressed Tom even more. When we finally arrived at the hospital on post, they wheeled me into an exam room. When the doctor came in, he asked if I was having any cramping. I told him no and asked, "Am I supposed too" He never answered but told me instead to just relax and lie back while the nurse and him proceeded to do whatever it is they do, during that time.

After he examined me, he told Tom and me we could go back home, everything was ok. He informed us the baby had been lying on my bladder for a while and I had been wetting on myself all night as sometimes happens with pregnancy. I was never so humiliated! You mean I went through all that just to hear I had wet on myself for several hours?

The doctor did tell us my blood pressure was extremely high and if I did not get it down, they would have to do a C-section. They asked if I had been following the eating program, they had given to me. I told them yes and added I had been sitting around with my feet elevated, too. Tom took me home and went back to his battalion.

Finally, one very early morning a day or two later, I wasn't feeling well and began having contractions. When I called the doctor's office later that morning, they told me to start timing them. They informed me when the contraction were every five minutes apart then I should come in.

The contractions were very uncomfortable, plus it took forever for them to get down to five minutes apart. It was more than twenty-four hours before I was taken to the OB unit at Silas B Hayes Hospital on base. Thank goodness Tom was home! He was a nervous wreck. He called my folks to let them know I was in labor and we were heading to the hospital. They drove down as soon as they heard. We were all extremely nervous.

When we finally arrived at the hospital, they took Tom and me back to a room, while my folks were on their way. When my folks arrived, Tom met them at the front gate to have passes made for them. The room I was in had a TV up in the corner of the wall that was blaring loudly. As the music from the show *Dallas* came on, I asked them to please turn it down, off would be better. I was having such horrible back labor. It felt like something was going to rip through my stomach any minute, just like you see in those horror movies. During this whole time, Tom would go back and forth, checking on me and letting my folks know how I was doing.

Actually, Tom didn't have to tell my folks how I was doing. They, and everyone else in that waiting room, could hear how I was doing with my extreme yelling. Yes, I was yelling. I was in so much pain and it seemed no one cared. While Tom was taking a break, this nurse came storming into my room, like she was in combat, with her hands full of her weaponry, which included a bed pan and tubing. She put her weaponry down next to the bed, reached over and flipped me on my side, and in a stern voice like a drill sergeant, said, "It is time for an enema" Then, while preparing her weapons, she started watching *Dallas* and even began getting a little excited. I don't know if her excitement came from torturing me or watching *Dallas*. All of a sudden, she said, "Oh girl, isn't that so and so who shot so and so?" With every ounce of my being, I flipped over and grabbed her arm. With this evil voice, which I had know idea where it came, I said, "I have had just about enough of your excitement, and if you don't get the heck out of here, I will take that hose and wrap it around your neck!" She grabbed her stuff and fled out the door. I knew then I had won that war.

At this time, I felt like I was in a combat zone. I felt bad of what I had just said and done, but I do not handle pain well. A few minutes later, the door flew open and the doctor, with anger in his voice and an angry look, yelled at me. "Ms. Burnes, you need to calm down. You are making all the other staff and laboring mothers upset." There again, with every ounce in me, I sat straight up, like Linda Blair in the movie *The Exorcist*, and with a deep, angry voice said, "Well, if you and the rest of the staff and mothers don't like it, get some ear plugs."

Just then, Tom came into the room, and the doctor looked at him and yelled, "Private! You better get your wife to at ease, like right now!" Tom said, "Yes, sir," while he saluted the doctor. The man left in a huff, slamming the door. Tom reassured me and mentioned that getting upset was just making it worse. "You need to relax," At this time, I was hurting so bad, so someone telling me to calm down was not what I wanted to hear. I think after twenty-six hours of labor and someone flipping you over to administer an enema while a TV show is blaring, well, you wouldn't feel like calming down either.

Just then I felt like pushing. Tom ran out into the hall and yelled for a nurse to come quickly. They quickly wheeled me down to the delivery room, telling me to do my Lamaze breathing and hold it. Really?! That's like telling someone when they are sick and have to relieve themselves to hold it; it's simply impossible. I don't care how much breathing you do. Once in the delivery room, they counted and told me when to push. I pushed and pushed so hard I ripped from back to front. I needed a tremendous amount of stitches.

After the delivery and while the doctor was stitching me up, Tom looked at me and said I could name our baby girl whatever I wanted. "Well," I said, "It is still April, even if it is the month of May." Then the doctor joked that her middle name could be May. I didn't find any humor in this since it was his incompetent staff that had told me I would be due in April. This whole military life was really getting to me, especially their unprofessionalism as medical staff.

They took April down to the nursery as Tom followed to where my folks could see their new grandbaby. I was wheeled down to recovery. Little did I know what was going to take place there. I was exhausted and real shaky. I felt like I delivered an eighteen pounder instead of an 8lb. 6oz. baby. I had lost a lot of blood, was very anemic, and was extremely weak. I felt like the life had been sucked right out of me.

As I am lying there, just resting and falling asleep, I felt this heavy pressure push down on my stomach with no warning. I came up flying with a first and punched that same drill sergeant nurse right where it counted. She must have had it in for me for some reason, coming in and pushing down on my stomach like that. I must have really ticked her off the first time around and this was her way of getting even with me. But she found out I could be at her level as well.

She picked herself up and told me she had to do that to rid the uterus of any excess blood clots. I glared at her and said, "That may be so, but you need to give a warning, not just feel free to come in and do as you please." She then told me I needed to get my lazy butt up and try to relieve my bladder to make sure it was working properly. Right then, that old demon side of me came out once again and with an angry, shaky voice I warned, "First of all, you do not talk to me that way. I don't know who you think you are, but I have had just about enough of your shenanigans. Enough is enough, and when I feel the urge to relieve myself, I will do so without any help from you, you got it?"

She left in a huff. I just wanted to go home so badly at this time. They would not take me to a room until I was able to relieve my bladder. I mustered up what little energy I had to go the restroom. It hurt and burned so bad that I just cried and gritted my teeth. After I was done, I made my way slowly to the hall and told a nurse that I had gone and that I was ready to go to my room. They wheeled me through the door to my room which was like a big dorm room. I had five other mothers to share it with. None of them said a thing.

They just stared at me like I was some kind of creature or something.

As I crawled into bed, my mom came in to see me. She immediately had this bewildered look on her face and exclaimed, "What in the world happened to your face?" I had no idea what she was talking about. She handed me the small mirror she always carried in her purse. When I looked, I let out this small, little yell and started to cry. No wonder those other mothers had stared at me! I looked like I had been worked over with a blunt object. All the other girls looked like they just stepped out of the beauty shop. Immediately, my mom asked one of the nurses if she could speak to the doctor. The nurse asked what the problem was, and my mother said they better have a good explanation why her daughter's face looked like she had been hit with a meat cleaver or somebody was going to have to pay heavily to fix it.

When the doctor came in, he told me and my mom that from pushing too soon and so hard my blood vessels had broken. He assured us that they would eventually fade, but if not, he said there was other options to correct it. I thought to myself "From what I have seen and have been through, I highly doubt I will let the military fix anything. Pay for it, yes, but I will go to an outside doctor before I'll let the army touch me."

My mom decided to stay for a week to help out. Dad went back home and would come back at a later date to pick her up. My dad was such a nervous wreck over this whole ordeal that I think he was anxious to get back home, plus he could not take any more time off work. I am so blessed to have a mom who stayed with me to help out.

I was in the hospital for a couple of days, which for me was too long. During my stay, I truly found out what the army meant when they told the soldiers if the army wanted them to have a wife, they would have issued one. Honestly, spouses then did not get treated well, especially after having a baby. Only if you were a high ranking officer's wife, did you get special treatment. When it was time to eat, they brought the food cart, left it in the hall, and then called over the intercom to let everyone know to get their own food trays. They also brought clean, folded bedding and lay it at the foot of the bed for you to change your own bedding. When it was feeding and changing time, the nursery would do their usual call over the intercom to let the mother's know, it was time to come and get your baby.

After I fed and changed April, I put her back in her bassinet where she fell asleep. I was feeling terribly sick and was running a fever. It seemed like every time I was feeding, I would get sick. It was the strangest thing. Just as I was trying to relax, that voice came over the intercom with its stern don't-give-a-darn tone instructing us that it was time to bring our babies back to the nursery. Well, I had just about had enough of this staff. I hit the call button and Ms. Whitchy Pooh came back with an ugly "Yes, what is it?" With the same tone of voice as hers, I explained that if she wanted those babies back to the nursery in such a timely manner, then she should come and get them herself. I also forewarned her that my baby was sleeping, and I was not feeling well at this time so I would bring her back to the nursery when I was good and ready. After that, I didn't even get a reply.

I told my mom about what was taking place with breast feeding and she told me the same thing had happened to her, with my sister and I. She and Tom left and came back with some bottles of infant formula made up in a little ice chest along with a bottle warmer. My mom started to warm up a bottle so it would be ready when April woke up. When she woke, my mom tried the bottle and she took to it very well. Both my mom and Tom asked if I had thought of a middle name or if April was going to even have one. I mentioned I had one in mind, and it wasn't May. I liked the sound of April Nicole. Both Tom and Mom agreed.

The next day I was able to go home. I couldn't have gotten out of there soon enough. I was so ecstatic. I am sure the hospital staff was just as ecstatic to see me leave as well. What a horrifying experience those five days at Silas B. Hayes. What I did take away from the turmoil I experienced, was a beautiful baby girl who was born on Memorial Day and a husband, mom and dad who stuck by me through one of my worst times. I felt very blessed and thankful for these people in my life, even though I was not the easiest to deal with.

Chapter 19

Baby Days and
Our Move to Base Housing

fter going through such a rough pregnancy and delivery, God totally blessed me with a wonderful little angel who made my life easier. I found myself waking up in the middle of the night reaching over to check if April was still breathing. She worried me because she frequently slept the whole night through; my mom even came in and checked on her. She was not a fussy baby. She would cry very little when she was hungry or needed to be changed. And, when you put her down for her nap, she would just lay there staring up at her mobile until she fell fast asleep. I was truly blessed with her being such an awesome baby. It gave me time to get rest and heal.

My mom being with me was a major help. Our landlord, Mrs. Bastanelli, came by with a baby gift. I told my mom that Mrs. Bastanelli knew Paul Anka personally, and that he was the one who lived in that big mansion on the hill you see when you turn off the freeway coming down the road to our street. My mom thought that was awesome because he was one of her favorite singers. Mrs. Bastanelli mentioned to my mother, "Well, Bonnie, maybe one of these days I will introduce you." My mom was so excited and replied that it would be an honor to meet him.

While we were visiting, I opened April's present and it was the most adorable little summer dress with matching bonnet and booties. My mom and I fell in love with it. Mrs. Bastanelli told us she had left the receipt just in case the outfit was too small or big so we could exchange it for a different size or something else. After she left, my mom asked if I felt up taking a ride to the children's shop and having lunch. Grandma wanted to pick up her new granddaughter some outfits. Tom was home that day so he said it would be nice for the both of us to get out of the house for a while, and it would let him have some daddy time since he was gone so much.

We located the children's shop and when my mom and I walked in, I remember both of us saying, "Oh my gosh, this is definitely not what I expected!" It sure was way classier than our children's shop, Hansen's. And the prices were definitely for the wealthy and elite. This children's shop had much more than baby clothes. It had tons of different baby furniture, things for moms-to-be, and everything and anything you could imagine for infants and children. The store even had a designer for nurseries and children's rooms. Mom bought a couple of things, but oh how we both wanted to buy more. We ended up eating at a really nice little restaurant within walking distance. I shared with Mom that I hoped Tom stayed stationed here because I loved Monterey and my favorite spot of all was Carmel.

That was my last day with Mom. The next day, my dad drove down to pick her up. I was so sad to see them go, and we all started crying. I told mom I would be up in a couple of weeks because Tom was going to be gone on maneuvers. As they drove away, I remember the hurt on their faces at having to leave their new grandbaby. My friend Carol had been right when she said my folks' attitude would change once their grandchild was born. I really enjoyed my mom staying with me and keeping me company while Tom was on duty. Both of my folks had a special place in my heart even if we did have our differences.

Our baby girl was getting so big and still had that wonderful disposition and sleep pattern. She was very content and happy. I felt bad for other mothers who lacked sleep and had fussy babies.

One day, my neighbor, Kathy, asked if I would like to take a walk to the bank with her. We gathered up the strollers, kids, diapers, snacks, and drinks. As we were walking, Kathy shared heart-to-heart about how her husband's work had slowed down and other things that were going on in their lives. Yet she never showed any signs of resentment and never spewed any anger from her voice. She stayed very humble while she confided in me.

"I truly wish I could be as calm and humble as you, Kathy," I stated. She smiled and told me eventually I would get there, to just keep trusting the Lord and praying because God works in all of us differently. She remarked, "He knows your heart. He already knows what's ahead and knows who will follow Him and who will not. It is all baby steps the whole way. It has been, and still is, a growing process for me and my family."

As we approached the bank, she said she was a little worried that their funds were not going to be so good, but she told me she fully trusted the Lord and He would take care of their needs. As I waited with the little munchkins outside at a little park by the bank, my heart really hurt for Kathy. I thought to myself, "Lord, make away for Kathy and Roman because they are so faithful to You." I would have helped anyone financially, especially our wonderful neighbors, but Tom being a private in the army meant our finances were very limited. Kathy had told me they always tithed and lived within their means, and no matter how limited their funds were, God always would show up in some way.

As I was sitting there waiting, I looked up and noticed Kathy walking towards us with tears in her eyes and a big smile on her face. When she reached me, she gave me a big hug and excitedly told me that God had been faithful to them again. She discovered they had an extra $200.00 in their account, and she wasn't sure how it had gotten there. She asked the bank teller to make sure that someone else's funds hadn't accidentally been put into the account by mistake. They did some checking and the teller said that nothing had been deposited into their account anytime that week. Kathy knew, however, how it ended up there; the Lord had His hand in it. She told me the extra $200.00 was exactly what they needed to pay for their utilities. She informed me that God had touched someone's heart who knew their situation or God had made it miraculously happen. With God anything is possible.

I was in such awe I called my Aunt Glenda when I got home and shared what had happened to our neighbors. She told me that since they were so faithful and trusted the Lord, He would continue to bless them. I truly began to see how, when you are faithful to God, He is faithful also. Like all those friends and family had said before, He never goes back on His word and He always keeps His promises.

One weekend that Tom had free, we decided to visit family in Livermore. A guy in Tom's unit, whom Tom and I had became good friends with as well as his wife, asked if they could stay at our house for the weekend. They had recently got an apartment, but the former occupants wouldn't be out until Saturday. Bill and Lea would be moving in that weekend but needed a place to stay. We said it would be fine since we were going to be back Sunday late afternoon anyway.

A couple of weeks went by and I went to do a little shopping at Weinstocks department store. When I was about to make my purchase at the register and gave the girl my card, she looked at me and smiled, and then told me there was something wrong with the card. She was on the phone for just a minute and the next thing I knew, security asked me to follow them to an office. I did not understand what was going on. They asked to see my driver's license, which I didn't have a problem with. They said there was a $200.00 charge on the card and then it had been called in stolen. I was confused. How did this happen? They pulled the purchase receipt, which had my signature but wasn't in my handwriting. I asked them to call me once they found out what had happened. In the meantime, I was going to do some of my own investigating.

Days went by before I received a call from the Weinstocks' manager who asked if I could come down to the store. Upon arriving, I was completely shocked at who they had found had used my card. They asked if I knew the woman who had forged my name. It was Lea. I said yes, and then they asked if I wanted to press charges. I was so upset and felt so betrayed by someone who claimed to be my friend. I told them no, but I would take care of it. They said if I changed my mind to let them know. I thanked them for all their help and stated I had a certain way I was going handle this. I would be confronting the source.

Later that evening, I mentioned to Tom what had happened with my Weinstocks card. "Are you going to approach Bill about his wife's actions?" I could not believe that we had given them the comfort of our home and they had helped

147

themselves like it was their own. I guess Lea thought our kindness also meant the comfort of using my credit card without asking permission. If she had asked me, I would have gladly let her use my card and she could have made the payments on her purchase.

Tom approached Bill the next day at work and Bill was totally beside himself. He apologized over and over about how sorry he was that Lea had pulled that. He also informed Tom he had caught her in many lies. Tom told him he was sorry for that fact and that I wasn't going to press charges on Lea, but I was still going to approach her about it. Bill wanted to talk to Lea first. I guess when Bill approached her about it, Lea had a sob story ready and tried to get him to believe her. I don't know what she said to Bill, but I do know he told Tom that Lea had issues and they needed to be dealt with by a professional.

A few days had passed, before I called Lea over for lunch. I knew she knew that it was over her forgery. When we sat down in the kitchen to eat, she started off with, "Well, Sandie, why don't you just say what you're going to say." I asked her straight up why she just didn't ask me. I would have let her charge my card if she needed something. I took every avenue with her, trying to find out why she had done it and how embarrassing it was for me to be approached by security on my own card. She didn't seem to feel to upset over it and told me I shouldn't be upset; she was going to pay the bill. I looked at her in dismay and told her that wasn't the issue, but, yes, she was going to pay the bill. She admitted she had found my card in my nightstand. I wondered what other personal items she went through in my home.

Lea also said if I decided to press charges, her dad would take care of it and all charges would be dropped. I thought, "Gosh, how vindictive and manipulating this girl is." She probably was right, however, because Lea's dad was a high rank on the Monterey police force and made people pretty fearful of him. According to Bill, he was a powerful man. I didn't know what that power was, and I really didn't care. Whatever the case, I just wanted her to pay the bill, and then wanted to keep my distance from her. I felt bad for Bill and Tom, but they, still remained friends.

Not too much longer after our ordeal with Lea, we received orders for base housing that Tom had put in for a long time before we moved into Monterey. Tom and I decided to move on base because it would be better financially for us. The base housing was brand new, and we were the first to move in. We really hated to leave our little white house and neighbors, but we planned to visit Kathy and Roman and the Bastanelli's from time to time, which we did.

At first, I didn't mind base housing. Truly, living on base did save us so much more money, but the drama from all the military wives was more than enough for me. I started really disliking it there. It seemed like everyone was talking about someone, plus Tom was gone more and more playing war or whatever it is soldiers do. I was lonely, even though April and I took more little road trips to Carmel with a friend who was a true friend or visited Kathy or the Bastanelli's. Yes, living on base was really wearing my spirit down.

One weekend, my folks came up to visit and asked if they could take April for a week. I was not too keen of being away from my baby for a week, not that she wasn't going to be well taken care of, but she had always been with me. The day my folks and April drove away, Tom and I had that same sad look, with tears rolling down our faces just like when my folks drove away the first time. The next morning, Tom left early as usual and I was lying in bed thinking of April, when all of a sudden, I heard footsteps coming up the hall.

I thought perhaps it was Tom and he must have forgotten something.

I called out to him, but there was no answer. The next thing I knew there was this thin, tall silhouette standing at the foot of my bed. The silhouette was the image of my friend Kari. I immediately knew something was wrong. I hadn't talked to her in a while. Kari had married a guy she had dated at Intel, and they had two children. Something down deep inside told me to call her.

I ran to the phone and called, but no answer. I knew my mom and Kari talked from time to time. I called my mom and asked if she had heard from Kari recently. She then mentioned that she had talked to her yesterday. The bad news was that her husband had taken the kids and all their stuff and now was in Oregon. My mom told me Kari planned to call me, but she was so distraught and dealing with trying to legally get her kids back. I knew they had been having marital problems, but I didn't think her husband would do something like this. I was so frantic for her that right then and there I started praying for her and the family. That day, I called all my Christian friends and family and asked them to please put Kari and her family on their prayer lists. I knew they would truly pray from the heart.

A couple of weeks had gone by before I heard from Kari. She told me the kids were back with her, that Dave had been arrested, and that things were working out well for them. The situation was calming down, and she felt at peace. Right then, I knew God had defiantly heard everyone's prayers. Yes, we do have a wonderful God who will intervene when we lift up others in prayer. I may not have been a true follower of Christ at that time, but one thing I knew for sure, He knew my heart and it was genuine.

Chapter 20

Tom's Orders
To Germany

s time passed, our friends one by one left Fort Ord with orders to Germany. One day, Tom came home for lunch with a bewildered look on his face. When I asked what was wrong, he informed me we would be moving to Germany. I was totally overtaken with the news. I was excited but also scared. Moving to a foreign country is a little nerve wracking, not knowing what to expect. Tom then said I should be excited. We had friends there, and it was my heritage. Like that was supposed to make it all better.

We moved back in with my folks until Tom left for Germany, which was about a week later. The plan was for April and I to follow as soon as he found a place to live and we received our orders.

The day my folks and I drove Tom to the Oakland airport, it was a very sad time for April and I. It was truly hard to say goodbye without a heavy heart and lots of tears. As he was boarding the plane, Tom said he would send for us as soon as he could. As weeks passed, I found myself writing more and more letters to Tom instead of calling. It was way too expensive for either of us to call. We only talked once a month, which was very rare because he was always out on maneuvers.

It took quite a while before Tom found a place for us and to get our orders. A lot of family and friends did not understand why it was taking so long. Well, when you are out playing army for weeks at a time, then come back for a couple of days just too go back out again, it doesn't give a person much time to look for a place, especially when they have to get their gear cleaned, trucks cleaned, and so on. Tom was good about sending money to help pay for April's and my stay with my folks though there was another comment about that as well because we did not get money as fast as we should have. People are always so negative on everything, especially when they don't understand or have not a clue what that other person is going through. Months went by and still no orders for April and me. I knew it would be awhile before Tommy could find a place for us to live because of all his military training.

Seven months passed before that one day when we finally got the call from Tom, that April and I had orders for Germany. As soon as I received them, it was a process to leave. We had to get passports and make sure we were up to date on our immunizations. As soon as everything was taken care of, and the packers had come to pack up our belongings, we were ready to leave the USA within a few days. April was now fifteen months and potty trained. Boy what a big relief for me. One less stress of having to deal with smelly diapers and changing during our flights.

The day April and I left for Germany was an emotional day as well, leaving my family and friends. We all cried so hard at the airport. All eyes stared at us while mascara was running down our cheeks and we were wiping snotty runny noses as well. It was a long flight. We flew from San Francisco to JFK in New York and had quite a layover. April and I were so tired and hungry. I rented a stroller, we ate, walked around a bit, then slept awhile. Finally, I heard the boarding call for our flight to Germany.

When we flew into Frankfurt and I stepped off the plane, I immediately experienced the difference between US airports and Germany's. Family was not there to greet you, you had politzi (German police) with uzis, and German shepherd's walking up and down the corridors. I had no clue where I was supposed to go or what to do, so I just followed everyone else and went through customs. I was so nervous and scared. I knew a little German, but not enough to get myself out of trouble if it came to that.

Walking out to the front of the airport I searched hard for Tom. It reminded me of when I would go to the Oakland coliseum for a concert, thousands of people everywhere. Everyone was calling out names for their family or friends. I held April so tight while searching for Tom. My heart was racing, tears filled my eyes, and my body was feeling just like my first roller coaster ride when you get that fear about the horrific speed and going through twist, turns, and upside down. Yes, that was how I was feeling.

Suddenly, I heard this voice in the distance yell, "Sandie, April!" I looked for the source of that voice and ahead in the distance I saw Tom. I was so focused on not letting him out of my sight I just blundered through the crowd not caring who I pushed or even knocked down. That was the first time I literally pushed people without any hesitation or even feeling rude or apologetic. All I cared about was getting to Tom and getting the heck out of this place. When Tom and I finally met, we all three embraced ever so tightly with all three of us sobbing tears of joy. Tom grabbed April and hugged her so tight with tears just rolling down his face. He said, "You have gotten so big. Daddy is so happy to see you and Mommy"!

Our drive to the city of Heilbronn was a long one but very beautiful. I couldn't believe how fast everyone, including Tom, was driving. Do they always drive this fast on the auto-bahn, that famous freeway?

When we arrived in the little town of Flein where our apartment was, I could not help but notice the cobble stone streets and the old buildings and houses with flower boxes hanging outside the windows. Everything was so pictur-esque like you would see in a travel magazine. There at the end of Weinburgastrase Street was this cute, little German house. We entered through a gate and walked through a beautiful garden up to a door where there stood an elderly gentleman with khaki shorts, a printed shirt, chubby cheeks, and a big smile on his face. Tommy introduced April and I to Jerschabech, and said in German, "This is my wife, Sandie, and daughter, April." Mr. Jerschabech gave April and me a very welcoming hug, then he led us through a corridor and up some stairs to our new home.

He told April and me in a strong German accent that he hoped we would like it here. I spoke back to him in German and said, "Thank you, you have a beautiful place."

Tom gave us a grand tour of our new home. It was nice, but everything was so different, nothing like I expected. The bedrooms had no closets; they had what the Germans call shrunks. They are kind of an armoire with drawers and a place to put your shoes. Older places like ours also had cabinetry hutches in the kitchens to hold your kitchenware and canned goods. The kitchen sink and bathtub had a tank mounted to the wall in which the water came from.

Our place was at the end of the street looking out over vineyards. April picked up on the German language quickly. Every morning, she walked out on our balcony, and if Mr. Jerschabech was down in the garden, she would peer through the railing and say, "Guten morgen, Jerschabech." He loved it when she spoke in German.

When I would bake or make certain dishes, I always took some down to Mr. Jerchabech, and he would occasionally bring us a bottle of German wine. I found out very soon my favorite wine was Affel Korn, an apple wine that tasted just like the green apple Jolly Rancher candy.

Our German neighbors across the street were super nice people. They always brought over fresh vegetables from their garden or homemade soups. They had two sons. One was in the military, so he wasn't there much of the time. The other son was around eighteen or nineteen and his name was Ulrich. We became good friends with Ulrich and his family. Ulrich had this cute, green Volkswagen Bug that brought back memories of my Love Bug.

One evening, I invited Ulrich over for tacos. He had never heard of them or had them, but did he ever like those tacos. I lost count of how many he had after the third one. Before he left for home, he told Tom and I he was going to be selling his car. I immediately told him I would buy it. Before Ulrich left, I sent some tacos with him so his folks could also try some. I was so excited about that green Love Bug I couldn't sleep.

But before I could drive, I had to pass the German driver's test. It took several tries for me to pass the test, learning all their signs. Getting a European driver's license is quite different than back in the US. It also is mandatory, that everyone who comes to Germany to stay has to take a head start class, which is a class you attend to learn basic German. To me, that was much easier than learning their road signs and driving.

I loved living in Germany and our little town. Although Tom was gone on maneuvers most of the time, I decided to take a part-time job on base and registered April in a preschool where she could socialize with other kids. I worked in a little mini mall doing car sales for the GIs. I will never forget my boss, Fred. He was Italian, very handsome, though not very tall, and drove a really nice Ferrari. There were a couple of other small car dealers also working in that little mall.

Also, right next to the car shop was a video store that was owned by a super nice German lady, Angie, who was married to a retired service man who ran and owned a liquor store on base. Angie and I became good friends; she would always let me know when a new movie was coming out so I could be the first to rent it.

My boss sold GMC and Harley Davidson motorcycles. The Ford man, Gino, who was also Italian, did not like Fred. Gino and Fred had something going on between the two of them. When Fred wasn't around, Gino would tear down the signs that I would hang up for GMC deals. He would walk right up to the front door and tear them down. I always hung them back up, but then he'd yank them down again. One time, he tore down a sign I had just hung, then told me I had better watch my back. I immediately called Fred and told him what Gino had said and done. Fred told me in his soft-spoken voice not to worry, he would take care of it. A couple of weeks went by and Gino started moving his stuff out of his office. I do not know what Fred said to him, but he was moving to a different area.

I met some super people while Tom was stationed in Heilbronn. There were some guys in Tom's unit who had wives or girlfriends, and we became like one big family.

Everyone gathered at our place for the holidays, and we had such a great time. We also watched each other's kids when someone had an appointment or had to work.

I became good friends with Master Sergeant Villalobos, who was the assistant to the Post Commander. Here is how we met. First, I need to mention that Germany's phone system had never been up graded. The country still had the old system where you would occasionally get a third party on the line, so when you dialed someone and were talking to them, you could hear another conversation from someone else.

I was working at the GM office, calling soldiers to let them know the status on their vehicle orders. I had called a battalion on base to speak to a Sgt. Amos about his order for his Harley. When the CQ answered the phone and said, "First berg aide Pvt. Johnson speaking," I asked him if I could speak to Sgt. Chris Amos. He then asked me to hold a minute while he called for him.

During this wait time, two other voices came on the line, a Lieutenant Red and Caption Hook speaking about transporting a missile. I was nervous because, if I could hear this, I am sure the bad guys could as well. And since the lines were not secure, these two officers should have known better than to be talking missions over this phone. I called out to them to let them know they were being heard, but they never answered. They just kept talking about the missile that they were transporting and the route they were taking.

I was really trying hard to get their attention when Sgt. Chris Amos came on the line. I asked him if he could hear the voices on his end of the phone; he told me just barely, but I could hear them very clearly. I asked him to please get his commander as it was an emergency. Seconds later, the commander came on the line, but the other party had hung up. I proceeded to let him know there was something very threating I had heard on his line and if he could meet me at my office or if I could meet him at the battalion to discuss what I had heard. He said he would be right there.

Not more than a few minutes passed, in walks the commander I had spoken with, along with MPs and the Post Commander. The Post Commander wanted to know exactly what I had heard on the phone. When I proceeded to tell them, I suggested that they need to re-route their missile mission because someone else could have heard it.

They interrogated me to the max. I was really getting upset and angry with them all. Here I was doing them a patriotic duty and they were treating me like I was an espionage spy or something. As they were walking out the door, one of the commanders told me not to tell anyone what was said and that they were going to take care of it. I swore I did not hear a thing.

Later that day is when I met Sergeant Villalobos. I guess the base commander told him what had taken place, and how upset and distraught I was. He sent Sgt. Villalobos over to meet with me and to cheer me up. Honestly, I felt so displaced at that time. Everyone who knew me had seen all the MPs and commanding officers walk into my office and the door shut. You know how people start gossip. Then, if that wasn't enough, rumors started that Sgt. Villalobos and I were having an affair because he was talking to me one day when April and I were doing our shopping on base. I had just about enough at this time.

Shortly thereafter, some of the other wives and I met at the recreation hall on base just to sit and chat while our husbands were out training. I had a little telephone book I carried in my purse with a bunch of family and friends addresses. Well, I guess I left it out while I was looking for something and someone had taken it. I did not notice it missing at the time. Little did I know, this person used my addresses to send chain letters. Guess who received one? My sister-in-law who hated me.

Tom's sister even went as far to take the letter to my folks and let them know just how much she hated me and now she hated me even more. My folks got upset and mad with her. My grandmother just happened to be there when everything took place and, being the hot tempered German she was, she had a very angry comeback, "I know there is an explanation for this, and how dare you come here and talk such hatefulness toward my granddaughter. She has never said one thing negative about you or your family." My mom told my sister-in-law she was overreacting over a chain letter, which people get all the time, and it was time for her to leave.

The next day, I received a call from my mom letting me know what had transpired. I was so upset with what Tom's sister had done, plus I had not sent the letter. My mom asked me how would I explain the German post mark. I told her to hold on a minute while I checked my purse, that's when I discovered my address book was gone. I then explained to my mom what I thought had happened, and that there probably would be more friends and family getting the same letter. Other people did, in fact, but no one else made such a big deal out of it. I mentioned I would drop Tom's sister a line to let her know what had taken place, but I wasn't sure it would make a difference because of her hatred towards me; she certainly wouldn't believe me.

My mom felt bad about all the crap I had to go through with certain members of Tom's family. I told her it was ok as long as Tom and I knew the truth, it really didn't matter what his family thought about me. Besides, I had other big issues to deal with, so her pettiness didn't mean a thing to me. But

I will admit I was very angry at her going to my folks and not contacting me personally about the matter.

Well, at this time I quit working for Fred and stayed away from base as much as I could. I had very little contact with some of the wives. There was just too much gossip going on; I really was struggling with it. April and I stayed at home and visited our friends who lived near us.

Everything I was going through with all the gossip was just another bump in the road with military life, and it was the beginning of more heartaches to come. But Sargent Villalobos always called to check on April and I, to see if we were ok. He sometimes came by to visit, and we would share about our lives. We became like a brother and sister to each other. He was married and had two boys I met; his wife and we would sit and talk for hours. It was nice to sit and be relaxed in conversation with others who were adults and had a listening ear. Sargent Villalobos and his wife shared a lot, and I was so amazed how strong the both of them were, especially for as long as they had been in the military and the things he had gone through in his career.

I heard his story of his time spent during war and before he met his wife. He proudly said she had a lot of back bone, and it takes a very strong and supportive women to be married to a soldier. He was right. That is how most of us make it through. It takes a strong-willed, kind-hearted woman with faith, hope, and love to be a soldier's wife. The soldiers too had to be there for each other during all those times, whether it be war or peace time. It is by our upholding each other through those bad and rough times that makes us stronger. As I left to go back to our empty apartment with just me and April, something hit me. I realized exactly what he meant and what his wife said. Yes, military life is a completely different life from the civilian world, and yes, we have to be strong with faith, hope and love for our soldiers, our families, and ourselves. I realized that all military need to hold each other up in every way we can and show respect.

It dawned on me that the reason I saw women who sat around and gossiped and had affairs with other soldiers is because they didn't have the qualities of being strong or supportive. Even the soldier who allows those things to happen to his fellow soldiers is very weak minded. Now I could see how the enemy comes into play with those who are as such.

Chapter 21

Living in Germany

I will never forget our first Christmas and winter in Germany. Winter in Germany is extremely cold with lots of lots of snow.

We headed out to look for an amazing Christmas tree because this was our first Christmas away from home and we had invited all our closest friends and their families for a Christmas Eve dinner. Tom and I searched for that perfect Christmas tree, but to no avail; we could not find one. I learned Christmas tree lots were not on every corner like at home. Germans did not put decorative trees in their homes, like us Americans. When you drove around and saw a lighted tree in a window, you then knew an American lived there. We came to the last tree lot and there were hardly any trees left but this one, sad, Charlie Brown tree all by its lonesome. I said to Tom and April, "This is the tree." Tom asked if I was sure, I told him once we decorated it and lit it up, it would be one of the most beautiful trees on the block. Of course, it

163

was going to be the only tree on the block because we were the only Americans on that street of Weinbergastrase, Flien.

We had a wonderful Christmas Eve dinner and a great time with all our friends. Everyone brought a dish and I supplied the turkey, mashed potatoes and gravy, and the desserts. I also had loaves of banana bread and zucchini bread wrapped festively. All the kids got to open one Christmas gift they'd brought from home. One of the gifts our daughter ripped open was a Glow Worm doll she had been wanting (they were very popular). The doll had a stuffed, green, worm-like body with a skin-colored plastic face that lit up. When you turned on a switch, it's face would have a dim glow, it was the perfect night light for children as they slept.

Now, all the guys in Tom's unit had given each other nick names. One of the guys, whose name was Bobby, had the nickname Bobby Cuckoo. I don't remember the story of how that name came about, but Bobby was kind of short and stout and had a cute, round face with rosy cheeks, just like the Glow Worm. The Glow Worm's name was now Bobby Cuckoo according to some of the guys

As everyone left that evening, I handed everyone their gift of wrapped breads, I was exhausted. At least I had no dirty dishes or anything to clean up; everyone had helped with that. We had a wonderful group of friends for sure. April was soon fast asleep holding her Bobby Cuckoo next to her with its little, round, glowing face. Tom and I sat on the couch to unwind with our glass of Affhel Korn, staring at our Charlie Brown tree, and reminiscing over how everything had turned out. Tom was off a couple of days, which was rare.

Early Christmas morning, and I mean early, I woke to the sound of this little voice saying, "Mama, wake up and open presents." As I slightly opened my eyes, the first thing I saw

staring me in the face was Bobby Cuckoo and a voice bub-
bling with excitement about opening presents. That morning
we just hung around as April played with her new toys and
tried on all her new clothes. I took baked goods in Christmas
baskets to our German neighbors and Mr. Jerschabech,
wishing everyone a Frohe Weihnachten (Merry Christmas)

After wards, we decided to visit our good friends, Paul
and Kathy, who were from Kentucky. I just loved their
Kentuckian accent. They, too, lived in Flein in a basement
apartment. I do have to mention that the older German
homes had old fashion key locks for every door in the house.
You did not want to lose or misplace your key for sure.

Kathy and I worked in the same little mini mall. She
worked with Angie in the video store. She always heard
everything that went on with Gino. Kathy and I were so
much alike. We were always getting ourselves into predicaments and become the talk of our husbands' unit, or should I
say, laugh of their unit. More like the laugh of the whole base.

On my way out the door with April, the phone rang. I
couldn't quite make out what the person was saying because
it sounded like they were crying and laughing at the same
time. I finally made out it was Kathy. She told me she was
locked in her bathroom. I asked how in the world she did
that. She proceeded to let me know she had been getting
ready to get in the tub, and she always locks the bathroom
door when she is by herself, she felt safer that way. She continued, saying she had forgotten her robe. When she got out
of the tub and over to the door, the key fell out of the lock,
bounced off her foot, and slid under the crack of the door.
She had been trying to use different things to grab it, but she
didn't have anything long enough to reach it. Thank goodness she had the phone with her. She had called her husband,
Paul, but he wasn't able to come to the rescue, so he was

leaving the house key at the front CQ desk with Sgt. Miller, and if I could run and pick it up. I told her I would be there as soon as I could and to just sit tight in a nice warm bath.

I headed into Heilbronn on post in my little, green Bug which didn't do too bad in the snow. As I pulled up in front of the battalion, Paul just happened to be walking out and he handed me the keys. All he could say was, "Leave it to my wife to do something so off the wall. Thank goodness she has you to come to her rescue."

As I headed back to Flein to rescue Kathy, I thought about the time a couple of weeks earlier when I had been Christmas shopping on base. I had our Toyota truck with the camper shell that had a door that would stick. I had put April in her seat in the cab and unloaded the Christmas gifts in the back, then went to pull the camper shell door down. It became stuck and so did my arm. I had a big heavy coat on, so my arm was really caught. I tried and tried to push the camper shell door back up with my free hand, but it was not working. I was way out in the parking lot, yelling for help and trying to jump up high enough to where someone could at least see my hand as I was yelling. April started crying, and I was getting nervous and crying myself. Here I was trying so hard to get my arm out and freezing at the same time. I was getting so exhausted from yelling, jumping up and down, and shaking from the freezing cold. Even though April was bundled up, I feared for her as well.

Then something came over me and I remembered what our neighbor in Monterey, Cathy, had told me about not fearing and trusting the Lord with all your heart; to let Him know you do fully trust Him and you know He will not forsake you. I remember calling out to Jesus, letting Him know I truly trusted that He would send someone to help. As I was calming myself and heavily talking to Jesus in prayer, a thin, tall man in uniform walked around the truck and introduced himself as Lieutenant Abrams. "I barely heard your yelling," he said, "but what caught my eye was your fingers rising above the shell. What I really heard was your daughter crying. I knew something was wrong, but I wasn't sure what all the commotion was." At that precise moment, I just started crying and thanking Jesus for sending this wonderful angel my way. I told Lieutenant Abrams the door was stuck along with my arm. I asked, before he helped me, if he could please grab my daughter and bring her to me so I could calm her down.

He grabbed April and handed her to me, and she calmed down right away. As Lieutenant Abrams was pushing the door trying to get my arm out, I could not help but notice he was the same lieutenant I had accidentally smacked in the face when I was giving someone directions on base. You see, I talk with my arms and hands a lot, and I had been giving directions to a lady on post. When I turned around to point in the direction she needed to go, my hand caught this man as he was walking behind me. I accidentally smacked him right on the right cheek! I was so embarrassed and told him I was terribly sorry. He just stopped. Rubbing his cheek, he reassured me he was ok, and commented that it would probably be in my best interest if I practiced giving directions with my hands down at my side when I turned, and then point. I apologized over and over. He stated again, that he was ok, but commented on how powerful my right hand swing was.

When Lieutenant Abrams finally released my arm, he stopped and kept looking at me. He finally asked if we had met before. I said, "Yes. Remember, I am the one who gave you the right hook to your right cheek." He started laughing and said he remembered. Before he walked away, I again apologized for smacking him and thanked him so heartedly for coming to my rescue. He smiled and gave April and me a big hug as we were parting ways. We both wished each other a Merry Christmas, and then he said, "Hopefully, if we ever meet again, it will be under better circumstances." I smiled and said, hopefully so. As I watched him walk away, I admitted to myself not all officers are arrogant and rude like some that I had run across, especially in Tom's unit.

I finally reached Kathy's and came to a stop. I was just about to get out and go rescue my friend, when all of a sudden, I felt this huge jerk and heard a loud crunch. I looked behind me and saw I had just been rear ended. Thank goodness I didn't have April with me. I had dropped her off at the day-care on base as I was leaving to bring the key to rescue my dear friend.

When I stepped out of the car, this gentleman driving a BMW got out, looked at the damage, and said some choice words in German. I could tell by the look on his face he was completely distraught about what had just happened. He had been coming around the corner, hit some ice, and slid right into me. He was so apologetic. I told him I was fine. He then reached in his pocket and handed me his card. Oh my gosh, the editor of the Heilbronn newspaper had plowed into me. He told me in German he would have his daughter call me this evening since she spoke English to let me know where to take my car to be fixed, and he would pay the bill.

He then left, as I headed downstairs to rescue my distressed friend. When I entered, I shouted it was me and I kicked the key back under the bathroom door. I waited in the kitchen until she finished getting ready. Kathy and I were to open shop that day, but she had called Angie to inform her what had taken place and we were going to be a tad bit late. I called the other Cathy, who also worked for Fred, to let everyone know the ordeal that happened. They both opened shop and stayed until both of us arrived. Thank goodness we worked for some understanding people.

While Kathy was getting ready, I told her what had just transpired out in front. She asked if the car was drivable. I told her it wasn't to bad and that the editor of the Heilbronn paper is the one who slid into me. She thought it was awesome that he was going to fix it.

Later that evening when I was fixing dinner, Tom walked in and told me he heard what had happened that morning. He started laughing, and said the whole battalion knew about it. I told him that Kathy was not going to be happy with Paul telling everyone. Tom said, "Hey, we all need a laugh every now and then, and you both are the base entertainers." As we sat down to eat dinner, the phone rang, it was the editor's daughter letting me know where to take my car. She gave me the address, which was a body shop there in Flein, and they would be expecting me. I thanked her for calling and asked her to tell her father thank you for being so kind and honest. I said it was very thoughtful of him and that blessings would come back to him.

I told Tom where I was to take the car tomorrow and since it wasn't far from home, I was taking April's stroller and we would walk back. The next morning, I dropped the VW off at the shop. The owner spoke very broken English, and he told me that I could pick my car up the next day. I told him how ever long he needed to keep it was ok by me. As I was putting April in her stroller, he asked if I needed a ride home. I explained I lived only a few blocks from the shop and the walk would be nice.

April and I headed home we made a few stops along the way to do a little shopping. I found this adorable, Bavarian-crochet dress that was just her size. She looked just like a little German girl with her blue eyes and blond hair, plus she could even say things in German; the dress just fit the image.

The next day I received a call from the body shop that my little green Love Bug was ready to pick up. I was so amazed at the workmanship; you could not even tell it had been hit. I told the guys they had done such beautiful work. I asked the owner if I owed anything, he said "No, as he gestured with his hand, it has all been taken care of."

I then went by a little shop in Flein and picked out a nice thank you card. I wrote in the card and baked a couple of loaves of banana bread. The next day I went by the Heilbronn newspaper station, took out the card the editor had given me, and asked the lady at the desk if I could see him. I couldn't pronounce his name, but she understood what I was trying to say. She left and a few seconds later the editor came out. He spoke no English, but I handed him the card and banana bread and told him, "Thank you for your kindness, thoughtfulness, and honesty. This is a little something to show my appreciation." I could only say bits and pieces in German, but I am sure he knew what I was trying to say. We gave each other a friendly hug before I left.

A couple of weeks later I got a call from my mom. She and my dad were planning a trip to come to Germany and stay for about a month. I was so excited! I immediately started planning all the things we were going to do when they came. This was going to be an awesome event for not only Tom, April, and me, but for my parents as well.

My Folks
Coming to Germany

I loved living in Germany, and really had grown to love the country and its people. The way the Germans lived and some of the things they did reminded me of my German family members back home.

I was blown away by the grocery stores. They were totally different than in the US. There wasn't an abundance of quantity. There were only three kinds of cereal instead of a whole aisle. Most of their condiments, like mayonnaise, mustard, and ketchup, were in tubes. The pickles and canned soups tasted just like grandma use to make. All their liquid beverages were in liters, such as milk, juice, cream, etc. Clothes and shoes were in metric sizes, which I had a very hard time getting use too.

The coolest thing was the grocery carts. They were kept in front of the store, lined up neatly. The carts were connected to each other by a small machine. You would put a mark in the slot which in turn released a small chain attached to the cart. When done shopping, you would put your cart back and reconnect the metal piece hooked to the chain back into the slot of the machine. It connected to the other cart, and then your mark was returned to you. It was like almost playing a slot machine. I started thinking what an awesome way this would be to get all the lazy people back home from leaving their shopping carts everywhere in the parking lots. The only difference between the Germans and Americans is that Germans are not wasteful like Americans. But instead of a $1.00, it would have to be like $3.00 to $5.00 dollars in quarters. Then watch how fast everyone would put their carts where they belong.

Germany also has mirrors where there are blind corners. They eating places are called "Guest Haus," which is like dinning in someone's home. You can bring your dog in the guest haus, as long as it is well behaved. All drinks are served at room temperature, and employees have a beer or wine break. Even McDonalds served beer. Nudity in Europe is not a big deal; it's even shown on commercials. Women no matter what age went topless at the pools or on the beach.

The whole time I lived in and traveled through this magnificent country, I saw so much beauty, cleanliness, and neatness even in the poorest of sections. There is a lot of pride in German culture on how they live. You never see junky cars or trash or anything of that nature laying about. We traveled to a lot of places, such as small towns, suburbs, and cities all around Germany, and they all were very clean and neat. I was fascinated by the big wooden barrels with down spouts from the house gutters that caught the rainwater, which the Germans used for watering their gardens and washing things down.

Businesses are totally different. The owner or employees start early in the morning, sweeping the sidewalks, curbs, and street gutters. They also close their businesses from noon until 2:00 p.m. Most people eat lunch and rest then. German breakfasts are continental, lunch is their main meal, and dinners are very light. People always walk. You always saw women early in the morning with their hand baskets walking to the delis to get their meats, breads, and eggs for the day.

Quite a few things took place before my folks came. I became very ill and, of course, Tom was gone on maneuvers for the hundredth time but was to return in a couple of days. I was really trying to hold out on going to the medics on base. Mr. Jerschabech checked on me and brought me soups and healing concoctions to make me feel better. He was such a wonderful, sweet man. My friends came and brought me things, and would take April for a while so I could get some rest.

Just before Tom and his battalion returned, my good friend, Kathy, took me to the medical clinic on base. By this time, I was very weak, running a fever of 102, and wheezing badly. I could barely breathe and, when I did, my lungs hurt so bad. They took my vitals, wrote me a prescription, and sent me on my way. Luckily, as I was taking my prescription to the pharmacy, Tom came walking in. He asked me what had happened. I could barely talk because I was wheezing so bad and could barely breath.

When I was ready to hand my prescription to the pharmacist, I looked down and saw it was written for Sudafed. I immediately went into a frenzy and started crying. Tom asked me what the problem was, as I was beginning to explain, a high ranking medical officer sat me in a wheel chair and wheeled me back to a room. He then informed Tom they were going to do x-rays and give me a breathing treatment along with an IV of antibiotics. The doctor really was angry with what had just taken place with my care. He was very angry with the staff. He reassured me I was going to be taken care of.

We came to find out I had pneumonia. I spent most of the day and into the evening being treated. Tom and April went to get something to eat at the cafeteria, and our good friends Paul and Kathy stayed with me until Tom came back. When Tom came back to the clinic with April, Kathy and Paul left for home and I was able to go as well. I was given strong antibiotics and told to get lots of rest, drink plenty of fluids, and to keep myself moving.

When we got home, I took a big swig of my cough medicine and fell asleep like a baby. The next day, I felt a little better than before, but I had a long road to recovery. Tom was home for a couple of days, which was nice, and he was a big help to me. Mr. Jerschabech came up to see how I was doing and brought us homemade soup with some brotchen (rolls). Tom gave him a loaf of zucchini bread and thanked him for watching out for us when he was gone. I finally started feeling much better as time went on.

After I had recovered, I received a call one day from one of the guys at the battalion letting me know that Tom had been mowing the lawn in front of the company which had a slope. His foot had slipped and went under the mower, and it dang near took his big toe off. I headed with April to the base clinic to pick up Tom. When I saw him with his toe all bandaged up and how peaked he was, I knew it was not good. He had several stitches, and they handed me a bunch of antibiotics and pain meds. There was no way he could get into a shoe or his army boot. He was going to be off duty for a few days, then be on light duty until his time off when my folks came. April had a little nurse kit so she would play nurse and take his temperature, check his heartbeat, and even share her Bobby Cuckoo with him to make things all better. His toe eventually healed, it actually took almost two months before he could wear those gross army boots like normal again.

One day on base, I was running my Beetle Bug through the car wash. As April and I were watching the soap spray and the brushes rotating toward the doors, she started yelling because they were scaring her. As I tried to calm her and let her know that they would keep going, I realized they were not moving. Those big brushes were just going around and around by the door and not moving. I instantly started to panic. I noticed two GIs from Tom's unit were walking in front of the car wash, so I thought if I honked the horn, I would get their attention and that of the car wash personal. I laid on my horn and believe me the sound of that horn would scare anyone, it had a very loud shocking sound. These GIs stood there facing me, and I tried to let them know with hand gestures that I was stuck. They already knew of my past predicaments, so they thought it would be fun to play along. They pointed at me, put their other hands behind their ears, and I could see their lips moving, saying in a smart way, "We can't hear you."

As they both started to laugh, the car wash personnel whipped around the corner in front of me and yelled, "Lady, you can go ahead and pull out." I thought to myself, "You mean all this time I was sitting here, being made a fool of while April and I were panicking, I could have just driven out." Well, I could just about imagine how this was going to make headline news on base. "Women gets stuck in car wash with child, doesn't realize she can just drive out." When I pulled out, I drove quickly off base and headed home completely embarrassed. I was hoping something like this had happen to others and I wasn't the only one.

My friend, Kathy, called and said Paul and Tom had heard about my episode at the car wash. News really travels fast on base, but it always did, when it concerned Kathy and I; we were the Lucille Balls of the Heilbronn Base. As we both started to laugh, Kathy then stated, "Remember when I locked myself in the bathroom? That spread like a wildfire." Talk about entertainment! Between Kathy and I, we sure kept the laughter and the moral up with our husbands and the rest of the battalion.

It had been about a year since we left home, and now my folks were coming to visit. They were going to be so surprised about how much their granddaughter had grown and changed. As we were waiting for my folks and watching for them at the airport, I mentioned to Tom that my poor dad was going to be a nervous wreck and overwhelmed when he stepped off that plane and saw all the politzi running around with uzis and German shepherds. I remember Tom making a statement, "Well, your dad should be used to it, as he is around nothing but Germans back home." He was right; it was no different than being around my high-strung, German family.

As soon as we spotted them, I could tell by the look on my dad's face he was scared. My mom was just fine. When my folks saw April, they started crying and could not believe how big she was. And my mom loved the fact she could speak some German. As we headed back to Heilbronn in our rental car, my dad and mom commented on how fast the Germans drove. My poor dad was beside himself and made the comment to Tom that maybe he better, slow down some because his butt cheeks were hugging the seat. We all laughed as other's passed us at the speed of lightning. After about the fifth exit we passed, my dad mentioned that Ausfahrt must be a big place because there were so many signs for it. We then mentioned to him, that wasn't a place; that was the word for exit. When we arrived home to our little apartment in Flein, Mr. Jershabech greeted us again at the door and we introduced him to my folks. My mom said in German, "Glad to meet you." As we made are way up to the apartment, my dad commented on what a nice view we had of the vineyards.

Tom still had a hurt toe, but his stitches were out. Tom had saved about three weeks' vacation for when my folks came so we could do a little traveling. My folks were going to be with us for about a month. The first couple of days, we just hung around the house and took them around Heilbronn, eating at some of our favorite guest hausas. My dad absolutely loved the fries. He commented how different they tasted compared to home. My mom loved the German beer and the Affle Korn wine.

On our European excursion we went to Austria, France, and Spain. My folks really enjoyed themselves seeing the sights. My dad was quite embarrassed walking along the boardwalk on the beach in Spain. He asked if all the women went topless. We told him that it was the culture in all of Europe. We bought little translation books for each place we visited. Most everyone was helpful, but I found that in France they were not. They did not like Americans too well, at least in the little French town we were in.

When we got back to Flein, we rested a couple of days before taking my folks to see the New Schwienstien Castle on the border of Germany and Switzerland. You had to walk up a steep mountaintop road to reach it. On your way up, there is a man who plays the accordion and yodels. We had such an enjoyable time touring the castle and learning its history. When we left, we took my folks to the Black Forrest and the largest cuckoo clock factory. There my folks bought the most beautiful grandfather clock, and had it shipped back to the States. It would more than likely be there when they returned home.

The following weekend we took my folks to see some more sights. We went up through all the little towns along the Rheine river. When the time came, it was beyond hard to see my folks leave. There were a lot of tears in saying our goodbyes. My folks really enjoyed their time spent in Germany, and so did we enjoy spending time and traveling with them. They had a lot to share with family and friends when they returned to the states. Not only would there be stories and pictures to share, but they were going to have a great piece of Germany waiting for them when they arrived.

Chapter 23

Leaving Germany and
Returning Home

fter my folks left, it was hard to get back into a routine again. Tom was back to duty full-time, and April and I were trying to adjust to no one being with us. I started feeling sick again, like I did when I was pregnant with April. I asked Kathy if she could watch April for a bit while I ran an errand to check something out.

I headed to the clinic on base to take a pregnancy test to see if my suspicions were right. When the nurse came out and told me that I wasn't pregnant, I knew right then, if they had prescribed Sudafed for pneumonia then they probably wouldn't know how to read a negative or positive pregnancy test. When I told them, I knew I was pregnant and that they need to do a blood test because it's more accurate, they reassured me it wasn't necessary; the urine test was accurate enough.

Then the doctor had me come back into a room to talk with him. He asked what made me think I was pregnant. I shared all my symptoms and told him they were the same as when I had been pregnant with my daughter. They wanted me to take another urine test. I could not believe they would repeat that, but then again this was the military and they seem to always do things that don't make sense about 99% of the time. The doctor doubted me. He said things like, "Maybe you want to be pregnant and just think you are. Maybe it is just a figment of your imagination." I honestly sat there in disbelief over what had come out of this man's mouth. I got up and walked out without taking another urine test.

I left there so angry. I had visions of me body slamming that doctor. I could not believe these military doctors. It was a running list of incompetence, first at Fort Ord in the states and now these circus clowns.

I had all the pregnancy symptoms and was even getting a little tummy pooch. I decided to go back to the states a little early because I sure in the heck did not want to have these so-called doctors anywhere near me when it was time to deliver. After all, these were the same docs that prescribed Sudafed when I had pneumonia. Tom understood, so he started the orders for April and I to go back to the states. In about three weeks April and I would be heading on that long flight home. Before we left, Tom and I decided to take a one last little day trip around the countryside stopping in little towns and touring the sights. I wanted to see a little more of Germany before going back to the States. Our friends, Paul and Kathy, came along with us.

We were having a fun, relaxing time until we entered one little town that had a beautiful water fountain right in the middle of the town's center. We decided to walk around and take some pictures by the fountain. As we were taking our photos, this older gentleman walked up to Kathy and told her and the rest of us in German that we Americans were not welcome here, so we should leave. As he spat on the ground in front of Kathy, I mentioned to Tom and Paul, "Let's just leave before they haul us away to some dungeon where no one will find us." I told the gentleman in German we hadn't intended any harm, but we were just admiring this beautiful little town. I continued, "But we will leave. God bless your day!" When I said that, his facial expressions softened, and a little smile crept across his face. As we drove away, I looked back at him and waved. He then returned this gesture with a wave and smile.

In order to prepare for our return to America, I went on base to the clinic to get copies of our medical records to hand carry back to the States. For some reason, this required, some kind of doctor approval. As I sat there and the doctor filled out the paperwork, he asked me how far along I was. I proceeded on being a smart butt and told him I wasn't pregnant, that it must be a figment of his imagination. Of course, he was not impressed with my comment.

After a couple of days, I finally received my orders to go home. I called my folks to let them know that April and I were coming back home a little earlier than planned, and that I would have to make frequent visits to the closest military base for OB checks. My folks seemed more excited about this pregnancy than the first. I was excited to get home, but I was also sad leaving Tom and all the wonderful people who had entered our lives. I told Mr. Jershabech and Ulrich that I would stay in touch; they were appreciative and said they would do the same.

I asked our good friend Doug if he would ride along with us so Tom would have someone to keep him company on the drive back to Heilbronn. When we arrived at the airport in Frankfurt, there again were a lot of tears from all of us. I told Tom I would call him as soon as we landed in the States. Then we headed through the airport toward our flight, passing the polizi with their uzis and German shepherds.

As the plane took off, my mind reflected back on the wonderful time spent in Germany. What an awesome opportunity it was to live in such a place and around those that were of my heritage. So many great people had entered our lives. I had the privilege of pinning Tom's sergeant stripes on while others received theirs as well. I adored watching our daughter learn another language, and the best part of that was when we stopped at the gate to enter the base, she would salute and say, "Move out, soldier."

It was a long flight from Germany to the East Coast of the US, and I was not feeling well. I was sick to my stomach. The stewardess was very kind to me, always checking and asking if there was anything I needed. Everyone was so impressed of how well-behaved April was on such a long flight. I always said to people that God blessed me with a little angel.

When we touched down in the States, we had a major layover at Kennedy Airport. I was still not feeling well, and April was starting to get cranky. I called my folks to let them know I was on US soil and would be heading home in about two hours. Home□that sounded like going to heaven in a couple of hours. I loved Germany, but it was a wonderful feeling being back in the States. I called Tom to let him know we were at Kennedy Airport and had a long layover. I told him I was not feeling well, and April was being a total cranky butt. I wasn't too upset with her since she had been so good on the whole flight. I couldn't expect any more from a four year old. I just did not want to hear any negative comments from anyone about how my daughter was acting.

Then a voice came over the intercom and said our flight to San Francisco was boarding. When I heard that, I said to April, "Well, kiddo, we are on our way to see Grandma and

Grandpa!" She calmed upon hearing that. To pass the time, April started pointing at my face and proceeded with our family tradition of "head bumper, eye winker, Tommy tinker, nose dropper, mouth eater, chin chopper, galley waters." That was something my Uncle Bob said when we were kids, so we had passed it down to our children.

Going from the East Coast to the West Coast seemed like a short trip compared to the overseas flight we had just been on. It was turning dusk, and as I stared out the window my mind drifted to that song lyric, "When the lights go down in the city and the sun shines on the Bay." I was once again thankful for my journey and for the footprints I had left behind. The best part of this journey was now having the comfortable road of memories to lead me back. I will never forget the wonderful, strong women friends I made during those times so far from home, and what we all had to endure with military life. They will always be near and dear to my heart.

Chapter 24

Our Life After Germany

When April and I returned to California, we lived with my folks until Tom's tour was finished in three months. Tom was not able to come home for the birth of our son, which was upsetting, but I totally understood. Our son, Greg, was born at the Navy base in Oakland, CA. It was a totally different experience than April's birth at Fort Ord. The care was great, and my delivery was much easier than with April.

Gregory was a small baby, only 6 lbs. 6 oz. Maybe that is why I had an easier time. I had a great group of nurses and the OB doctor was awesome. They were always checking me while I labored and gave me something to relax me some. They spoke a lot calmer towards me, instead of being rude like at Silas B Hayes. Let's just face it, they were more professional as a medical staff.

Greg and April were like day and night. Greg was just horrible; he woke every two hours for feeding and never was content unless he was being held. I spent so much money buying everything imaginable to keep him entertained, but nothing worked. However, the minute you picked him up and held and rocked him, he was fine. I could not get nothing done and it was frustrating for me. My mom told me to just put him in his play pen and let him fuss for a while; he would soon figure it out. I was not use to Greg's kind of fussiness since April had been so content with anything and everything. After a few times letting him fuss without running to pick him up, he eventually figured it out.

It was drawing near to the time Tom would be on that big ole Jet airliner heading home. I was getting very excited for that day when I got the call from him just a week before his final trip home that there had been a bombing in one of the towns in Germany at a disco tech, and now they were put on a full alert in case of a terrorist attack and possible war. I was totally scared for him and everyone. Another couple of weeks went by and I hadn't heard anything from Tom. I was always listening to the news and would contact other army friends to find out the status if Germany had gone to war or not. Thank goodness we hadn't. But I still hadn't heard from Tom.

Finally, a week later I received a call from Tom that he was on his way home. They hadn't been allowed to contact anyone with all the chaos over the bombing. It was about four months after Greg was born that Tom returned home from duty. He had served eight and a half years active in the Army and two years in the National Guard. The plan was to wait 6 months, then he would sign back up in the army and finish his remainder time on retirement and getting into the MOS of his choice, not the army's.

We moved to Union City where Tom started working for a small trucking company. We rented a nice town house in a gated community. We couldn't afford day care at the time, so I worked graveyard shift at a 7-11 convenience store. My shift started at 11:00 p.m. and ended at 7:00 a.m. Tom and I barely saw each other because he worked days; we passed each other at the door early in the morning. I would be just getting home and Tom would be leaving. It was like living the military life once again. Usually, I took a short nap when the kids took theirs. I then got dinner ready, after we ate, I went to bed to sleep for about three to four hours while Tom cleaned up and got the kids ready for bed. Then he would wake me. Boy, what a life!

After working at 7-11 for a while, I found out why the other girl quit. I was informed by another employee that she had been robbed and the guy had drug her around the store by her hair as he filled his bag with items off the shelves. Once I found this out, I was concerned my life might be threatened, so I started to apply for other jobs. In the meantime, I went to work with a can of Raid, and a small, short, solid baseball bat Tom had bought me.

One night while I was taking out the trash, I heard this awful female scream. As I tried to adjust my eyes and search for the direction of the scream, I saw across the field two silhouettes running. To me, it looked as if someone was chasing the other while the other was screaming for help. I was getting nervous for the girl, so I ran back in the store and called 911. I was dumbfounded by the questions the dispatcher asked. Here it was 2:00 a.m. and she was asking me what the people were wearing and what direction they were running. I told her just send someone fast, please, before the woman ended up dead. I told her I was at the Alvarado 7-11 in the canyon.

I hung up the phone and ran back outside with my can of Raid and baseball bat. All I heard was dead silence. My heart was racing, as I had all these thoughts running through my head wondering what had happened. I was so upset at this point. If only the woman had run toward the store, I could have helped her. I would have used my Raid and bat on him. Fifteen to twenty minutes went by and still no police. When thirty minutes had passed, I was ready to call 911 again when the phone rang. A woman's voice came on the phone and she asked if I had called the police. I answered her yes, but that it had been a while and the poor girl in danger was probably dead. She told me the police were at her 7-11 store which was about half an hour from where I was. "How did they end up there?" I asked. She said I gave 911 the Alvarado store instead of the Alvarado Niles store. I was dumb founded; I did not realize that Alvarado turned into Alvarado Niles. The woman told me the police were on their way.

I hung up the phone and started to cry. My stomach was hurting, and all I could think about was the police finding the woman out back dead. As I was waiting, here comes two police cars with their spotlights on; one went one direction and the other another. Ten minutes later, both officers came in the store. I asked them if they had seen or found any-thing. They both asked me questions. When they were done, I finally said, "Well, did you even bother to look if there was a freshly dug grave? That is a lot of field out there and, since an hour has gone by, he's had enough time to dig a hole and throw her in it." They both looked at each other and grinned. One started to laugh and the other turned to me and said, "Ma'am I think you watch too much TV." I was so appalled by that comment I didn't even offer them a cup of coffee or a doughnut.

In the early morning hours, it was routine for a lot of the commuters to stop in to get their coffee and whatever else they wanted. I had my morning rush as usual after this crazy night, as I made more fresh coffee, fill the dispensers, and get the store ready for the crowd. A short while later, as I was getting things ready before I left, I noticed this young man come into the store and walk around looking. I will admit, he made me feel uneasy. I walked behind the counter where I kept my can of Raid ready along with my handy-dandy, small-grip baseball bat. I tried to not look obvious, but he was really freaking me out.

Just as I was about to ask him, if there was something I could help him with, some people walked into the store. As they left and got in their cars, the young man walked up to the counter and quietly asked me if I believed in Jesus. I stood there thinking to myself, "If I answer yes, he might kill me." I also thought how strange of him to ask me that, especially given the night I had just gone through. I asked him if it was a trick question while I had one hand clinging to the Raid and one on the bat under the counter. I confidently looked directly at him and answered, "Yes, I believe." He smiled and said very calmly, "That is wonderful," and then walked out the door.

As I was watching him walk across the parking lot toward the field, our day shift person came in. I started telling him about the gentleman who had just left and how strange he acted. I looked up to point to him, but as I looked in the direction he had been walking, he was gone. I ran towards the door and outside to look for him, and he was nowhere. I asked the day employee if he had seen a young man walking as he pulled up. He said he hadn't seen anyone.

I was totally in awe with what had happened. I wondered if somehow what had happened last night and if this man were connected in some way. Maybe I was having a spiritual battle at that time. I don't know why I thought this, but it just seemed so odd that this young guy would ask me

189

such a question about Jesus, if I believed or not, and then simply disappear when he left the store. The next three days I was off from work and I searched for some answers for what had happened. I read my Bible and hopped I would find something that would maybe explain the situation. Of course, nothing I read made any sense because I didn't have that strong a relationship with the Lord and His Word. Of course, I wouldn't understand. I thought later I would talk to my Aunt Glenda about it; she was of strong faith, and maybe she could explain it and enlighten me on what I had experienced.

A little later that morning, our little neighbor girl, Erin, came by to play with April. Erin frequently came by, but the last couple of months she came by more and more and always wanted to stay. She was quiet and somewhat shy, but she wasn't shy when it came, to helping herself in the kitchen without asking. Her mom worked days and her dad worked nights. I thought she never wanted to go home because she was an only child and enjoyed playing with kids. Most of the time, she asked if she could stay for dinner. If her dad came to pick her up, she would beg me if she could stay a little longer, which I had no problem with. The minute her mom pulled up from work, however, she would smile and say, "My mom is home," and run out the door. I always thought something was wrong with that picture, but Erin never looked abused. Then I thought maybe her dad verbally abused her and that was why she acted the way she did.

I asked April when she played with Erin if her friend said anything about her parents. She replied, "No." I decided to keep my ears and eyes more open to what is going on with Erin's family. A couple of days went by and Erin didn't come over and we did not see her or her folks. I decided to walk over with the kids and knocked on the door, but no answer.

I hadn't seen the mother either coming or going, which I considered to be strange. I thought about calling the police to just come and check, but I thought I probably would get those same two officers and they would have some smart remark. Instead, I walked to the complex office and asked the office manager if she had seen or knew if Alice, David, and Erin were gone on vacation or something. She told me Erin and her mom had left the other day to stay with Alice's mother. I asked where Dave was, and she told me the police had arrested him. She wasn't sure why.

A few days passed and I was cleaning house when I heard a knock on the door. There stood Erin and her mom. Alice asked if Erin could stay for a few hours because she had some business to attend too. I told her, it was fine and that if Erin needed to stay longer, it was ok. Alice broke down crying. I offered for her to come in for a bit. Taking me up on the invitation, Alice proceeded to tell me that Erin was being molested by her dad. I instantly felt so shaky and started to cry along with Alice. I asked, "Do you know how long this has been going on?" She wasn't sure. I thought to myself, "Why, Sandie, did you not see the signs when Erin always wanted to stay, and how she begged you to let her stay longer when her dad came to pick her up?" I felt sick to my stomach and anger built up inside me because April used to go and play with Erin at her house. But April was a very bold, sassy girl. I know she would have told me if something had happened to her.

I told Alice as she was leaving that if she ever needed anything, please don't hesitate to ask. We gave each other a hug and I wished her well. I told her I would pray for her and Erin. As she drove away, I could see the hurt and bewilderment in her eyes. My heart felt so heavy, for the both of them. That poor girl and what she has been through!

When Tom got home from work, he saw Erin was back and was staying for dinner. "Where have you been, young lady?" he asked with a smile. Erin replied that her and her mom had been staying with her grandma. Tom said, "Oh! Grandma's house is always a fun place to be." Then April popped up and said, "Yeah, I love to go to my Nana and Papa's house." Just about the time Tom was going to ask Erin about her dad, I popped up and changed the subject, asking Tom how things had gone at work that day.

Tom told me he wanted me to put my notice in at work because it just wasn't safe. I asked him how we were going to afford it, and he told me he was getting a raise at the trucking company. I put my two weeks' notice in, and the manager wasn't too happy about me leaving. He made me feel guilty, but I told him I needed to be home with my kids more. It makes me angry toward people who make you feel guilty and then you have to explain yourself to them. It wasn't until later in my life and my walk with Jesus that I realized you don't have to explain yourself to anyone but the Lord, and He already knows before you even take it to Him.

Months before Tom got the trucking job and prior to him getting a raise, he and I both had put our applications in at the Lawrence Livermore Lab where my dad worked. The Lab paid well and had great benefits. We both applied with a company called Flore Daniels, which was contracted through the Lab.

Finally, the call came that Tom and I were hired. I was so excited because it was a good job (so I thought). Now I had to find a sitter close by whom I could trust. Tom and I were now going to have to commute from Union City to Livermore. That was going to be an ordeal within itself.

It took only a week of commuting before Tom and I started to look for a place closer to live. The commute was treacherous, and so was our schedule. We got up at 4:00 a.m., made sure the kids were ready to go, and left the house at 5:45 a.m. Next, it was drop kids off at day care by 6:00 a.m. and be to work by 7:00 a.m. We got off at 5:00 p.m. and picked kids up between 6:00 and 6:15 p.m. depending on the traffic. We usually had our dinner around 7:00 p.m. Then it was bath time for the kiddos and then bed. Tom and I took our showers and got in bed by 9:00 pm. The whole routine started all over again at 4:00 in the morning. This got old quick.

We couldn't find anything in Livermore that was reasonable, so we moved to Tracy. It was only, a thirty minute commute, but it was in traffic as well. Commuting seems the way of life in California. You couldn't get away from that commute traffic no matter where you lived. We found a nice, cute duplex with a fenced back yard on a quiet street. Tracy is where April started school and Greg had a wonderful day care.

As we drove away from our quiet, gated community, many thoughts assailed me. I could not help but think of poor, little Erin and her mother. I knew they had a long road of healing ahead of them. I still wonder about that night at the 7-11 and the mysterious man who approached me and then was gone. Was it a spiritual test, or was I going crazy, or I did watch too much TV? My mind always drifted and thought of the what if's.

Chapter 25

Our New Journey
with a New Job

fter we moved into our spacious new place and started our new jobs, things were going well. The kids had an awesome sitter and we had some really nice, next door neighbors. Dee and I became friends and did a lot together, including crafting. We made wreaths of all sorts and some flower arrangements in vases. Her girls and my children went to the same school, and then she and I started going to church with the kids (it was non-denominational). Our husbands never went, but that was ok. We did not ever pressure them about going, but we hoped they might eventually join us.

I am so glad I went, and also that my kids took interest in it. Our pastor looked a lot like the singer Kenny Rogers. I laugh because I think most of the congregation went because he did look like someone famous, not because they were interested in learning about Jesus. I am sure some were there to learn and truly seek the Lord, but from what I saw and heard, very few wanted to learn the Word. Most were always making comments about someone else on what they were wearing or who did what.

My daughter started going to Pioneer Girls and loved it. As time went on, not only was she involved with Pioneer Girls, she was also into dance and baton. And then both kids wanted to join karate. Tom and I were all for our kids being active, but it was getting to be too much. We had no time for home life. It was busy, running home after work to eat a quick bite, and then off again and running till 8 o'clock at night. It wore us all to the edge. April stayed in Pioneer Girls for a while, and both continued karate. April decided to quit Karate and Pioneer Girls. She now had a new interest.

She and a friend decided they wanted to join Girl Scouts. I was excited to hear that and told April I had been in Blue Birds, Brownies, and Jr. Girl Scouts when I was younger. I had a lot of fun selling cookies and doing certain activities to get a badge or a pin on my sash. April got even more excited when I told her I received a lot of patches and pins. I shared, that in Girl Scouts you get to learn how to do all kinds of rewarding things. So off we and her new friend and her mother went to sign up.

As Sally and I were signing up the girls, one of the administration ladies asked if we would like to volunteer to lead the group in our area. We said sure not realizing what we were getting ourselves into. After about two months of running home from work and getting to the meetings, plus having all our Saturdays tied up with activates and short trips for the girls to earn their merits, it got tiresome and old. Sally and I often heard complaints from parents about how we should and should not be doing certain things. After being criticized several times by some of the others, who were stay-at-home moms, Sally and I had enough and told them we were going to step down from being group leaders. We suggested that those who did not work and had more time on their hands could step up to the plate and be leaders since they knew everything about being a top-notch Girl Scout leader. Boy, you could have heard a pin drop in the resulting silence. And guess what? All those biddies who complained constantly, well, not one offered to help out.

Sally and I told the Girl Scout Council we were truly sorry that we were not going to be there as leaders anymore. We also informed the girls that the council would find someone willing to do the job. We felt bad for all the girls because they really enjoyed their scouting. It had taught them how to work together as team players.

One Sunday evening, Tom's super good friend, Pat, who he had grown up with, had dinner with us while his wife was out of town. We had a great visit with him, and invited him and his wife, Peggy, over the following weekend for a barbeque. The plans were happily set.

The next morning, we followed our usual routine of getting up for work and the sitters. Early that afternoon, however, my boss, Ginny, came to me and quietly said, "Your husband is on the phone and he sounds really upset." I quickly answered the phone. Tommy was crying and could barely talk. When I asked what was wrong, he told me Pat had been killed in an accident. I was in total shock! My heart felt so heavy with grief as I started crying. How can this be? He just had dinner with us the night before.

We both left work and headed home. I immediately called Peggy and got no answer, so Tom called Pat's mom and spoke to her for a bit. His mom was devastated. Tom asked if she had heard from Peggy. Margaret said Peggy was heading with Marv, Pat's brother, to identify him. My heart hurt so bad for Pat's family. We had grown so fond of Peggy too. Thank goodness they had no children. Worse, my heart ached heavily for Tom. Pat and him, were best pals; they did a lot together and had shared a lot of memories. I still was in a state of shock because we had just seen him. It just goes to show that, no matter what time of your life, you are never promised tomorrow. Tragedy can always strike.

We later found out that Pat had been leaving a place he delivered a load and was picking up speed to get out to the highway. A tarp that was laying in the road flew up under his truck and wrapped around an axle. The truck locked up and the cab twisted around to its side and jerked which caused him to fly out the window. He died instantly.

After the funeral, we went by Pat's mom's home to give our condolences to the family. We stayed in touch with Peggy. She knew we would always be there for her. Tom and I would always go by to help her with anything she needed done or fixed around the house, and we would always have her come by for dinner or just to hang out.

After summer passed with all its vacations to see family and friends, it was time for all of us to get back into the routine of work and school. A new girl named Patty started in my department. She seemed very nice and was always sharing her faith. Everyone seemed to like her, but, in a very short time, me and my co-workers found out she was a wolf in sheep's clothing. She started a lot of trouble in the workplace. Our main boss, Jenny, was never around when everything with Patty took place. She was always in her office taking care of paperwork, so she did not have a clue what was going on. Every time Patty went to Jenny with her latest lie, Jenny believed her.

One day our lead, Doris, Patty, and I were washing the glassware the chemist used, and Patty kept getting all kinds of phone calls from her friends. On the last call, Doris told

Patty she needed to let her friends know they should only call on her lunch time. As soon as Doris said that to her, Patty grabbed one of the cylinders and raised it like she was going to hit Doris with it. As soon as she raised that cylinder, I immediately grabbed her arm and mentioned she better not even think about it. Patty yelled and threw it in the sink where there was a lot of other glassware. All of it busted into pieces.

Just about that time, Patty walked out and Jenny came in wondering what all the commotion was. Doris told her what had happened. A few minutes later, here comes Patty all upset because, as she said, Doris had told her she could not use the phone. Doris and I both blurted out that was not what was said. I could not believe the words that came out of Patty's mouth then. She made Doris and I look like total fools. She stood right there crying and putting on the most pitiful lying act ever.

Right then, I remember what my Aunt Glenda had said to me about watching out for wolves in sheep's clothing. I understood the whole concept in that moment. But our boss did not see it. After that, I kept a keen eye on Patty. If she only knew how foolish she really looked.

As days passed after the incident with Patty, Jenny assigned me to do the autoclaving for the week. The lab had this enormous autoclave that was about ten feet deep and about six feet high. It had different settings for whatever materials you were autoclaving that day. It mainly was used for autoclaving Sharps containers, waste materials, and sterilizing glassware.

I had just set all the settings on the autoclave to get it ready for the next run before I went to the storeroom to grab some things. While I was in there, I heard Patty and someone else walk in behind me talking. I stood real quite behind a shelf where they could not see me. I overheard Patty tell this other person that she was going to make sure that I would not get the position she applied for. "I'm going to make sure of that," she said.

When they left, I proceeded with my normal routine. I casually walked back into the lab and loaded the autoclave. When I looked up at the control knobs to get it started, I realized all of them had been changed from their proper setting which would have caused a major catastrophe. If that would have happened, I would have been in a whole lot of deep trouble and probably would have ended up losing my job. I calmly switched the knobs back to where I originally had set them. Patty did not see that I corrected the settings. When the autoclaving was done and had gone smoothly, I walked up to her and said, "By the way, you set the control panel wrong. I doubled checked before I started it."

Later that morning, as I was getting things ready for the next run of glassware, I happened to glance into the storeroom and there stood the queen of damnation staring at me with a very hateful look and evil eye, so I gave her the "up yours" gesture with my arm. Naturally, she ran to Ginny to let her know what I had done. A few minutes into finishing up with the glassware, here comes Ginny and Patty. Ginny preceded to ask me why I made a gesture to Patty. Without any hesitation, I played the same game Patty did with everyone else. I smiled and looked at Patty and said, "Now, Patty. You know that was a figment of your imagination." You could see the anger build up inside of her. I knew I could play that game the same as her.

When the open position working with the chemists that I had applied for was finalized, the head of the department, Bill, came into the room and we all gathered round the table to hear who had the new role. When Bill was about to announce who got the title, I instantly said to myself, "And the winner is...." As the drum roll played in my mind, Patty and I gave each other the stink eye. My heart was pounding. Then Bill announced that I had the new position! I will never forget the evilness that came across Patty's face. You know that old expression, "if looks could kill?" Well, if they could have, I truly would have been dead. Everyone was excited for me except Patty. This new position also meant I would have very limited contact with her, if any.

It seems right after I started working the new job, which I truly enjoyed, things started going haywire with certain chemists and other lab personnel that I worked with. Things started missing that I needed for my responsibilities, and I there were false accusations against me. I had a notebook in which I kept all my notes on the contaminated soil I was working with for the environmental department. Some of my pages end up missing out of the book, so they accused me of falsifying data since those pages were missing. I was totally heart stricken, so I decided to leave.

Before leaving I had a meeting with the bosses and told them all no matter what they thought about me or if it they were taking the word of someone without fully investigating, eventually everything was going to backfire. You know that old saying "what goes around comes around?" Well, the truth always prevails. I also told them that accusing without having factual evidence was not good, and before anyone starts pointing fingers at me, they better make sure their hands are clean. All I got from them was blank stares and silence. They all left except for Barry, my main boss. He was very displeased with the outcome from everyone there and told me I was an excellent employee, and I could use him as a reference for any future jobs. I thanked him and told him he was a great boss and thanked him for believing in me. We then shook hands and then I left the premises never looking back.

I guess God was teaching me a very valuable lesson about people and how the enemy can use them against you. The other lesson He was teaching me was how to handle these situations in a spiritual way, but I hadn't quite reached that chapter in my life just yet. Looking back, I can honestly say there was a lot of truth behind what my Christian friends and my aunt and uncle said to me earlier in my life about wolves in sheep's clothing and how they are very good with fooling so many. I truly was beginning to see what they meant by that statement.

I did find out that later Patty was put in another position working in a room all by herself. I know that must have driven her crazy because she did not have anyone to place blame on. I guess God taught her a valuable lesson as well. You cannot get over on anything when it comes to God. He sees and knows everything. He is the judge and jury, and when you think you are fooling everyone around you, you are truly fooling yourself. You have to pay the consequences, even if it means being separated from others and put in a room all by one's self.

Chapter 26

Our Roller Coaster Ride with Family and Friends

After all the turmoil at the lab, so many other interruptions kept coming our way in our life and marriage. Not only did Tom lose a close friend, but we were betrayed by so many, including friends and some family. Our marriage of ten years was dwindling, Tom was off in his own little world, and certain family were always giving advice, especially the ones who could not even get their own life together. Isn't it funny how others can always find fault, but never see their own. I guess we are all guilty of that. But at the time, no one sees that. Betrayal and lies were surfacing with so many around us. It seemed like my roller coaster car was derailing from the track.

I was having all kinds of gallbladder issues and had a hellacious gallbladder attack at work. I was sent right away to see a specialist, and within that week my gallbladder was removed. It was a same day surgery. Tom and my parents were there with me. I was so thankful I had such a great doctor who did not let me continue on with the pain.

After we left the hospital, I told everyone I was starving since I hadn't eaten for twenty-four hours or so. We stopped at a nearby restaurant that had a jukebox. As we were waiting for our food, April asked her dad if he would go up with her and pick a song. Tom pulled out some change and they both were getting ready to hit the jukebox when our son, Greg, said, "Dad, play, *'Once Bitten, Twice Shy Baby.'*" My folks laughed and said, "Oh Gregory, what kind of song is that?" He said, "You'll see, Grams and Pop!"

Turns out someone beat them to the jukebox and the song, *Ice, Ice, Baby*, started to play. April was only around six years old, and definitely not shy of anything. She then started dancing and singing the song. Everyone watched her as she did her dance impression; some even joined in and clapped along with the beat. After the song ended, everyone clapped. When she sat back down, we said, "Wow, April, those were some awesome moves you made out there." Her reply was, "Yep, it sure was." Our daughter was so bold and sassy, and loved her music and dance, just like her mama.

For her seventh birthday, we surprised her with tickets to see New Kids On The Block who were coming to the Oakland Coliseum where my folks had taken me and my sister when we were growing up to see Disney on Ice; the famous Olympic ice skaters Peggy Fleming and Dorothy Hamill; the famous basketball team, the Harlem Globetrotters. It's also where I spent my teenage years seeing my favorite singing groups. April was so ecstatic; New Kids On The Block was one of her favorites, perhaps only second to Michael Jackson.

Let me interrupt myself to share a Michael Jackson story here. I will always be grateful to my boss, Doris, whose son was a lights and camera man for a lot of celebrity entertainers.

He traveled mostly with Michael Jackson and Tina Turner. He said they were his favorites to go on tour with because they were real people and not fake. They would sit with the crew and visit when they had a lunch break. On one particular tour with Michael, Doris's son told Michael about April and that he wanted to bring back something with Michael's signature. April received a picture that said, "To April, one of my biggest fans, Love Michael Jackson" and one of his stage towels that he signed as well. April had that towel for many years and used it as her bath towel. I told her that by using it over and over and washing it all the time, Michael's signature was going to fade. She did not care. In her mind, she thought by using it, she was going to become a great dancer just like him.

Back to the New Kids and our big night. I admit, those boys put on one heck of a show despite a whole coliseum of screaming girls. There was a dad standing next to me with his daughter, and when I looked up, he had cotton balls stuck in his ears. I tapped him on the shoulder and yelled, "Do you by chance have any extra cotton balls?" He laughed, reached in his pocket, and pulled out a large baggy full of them. I don't know how many I stuck in my ears, but they did form a little bit of a sound barrier.

I have to say going to that concert, even if it was just for one night, took me to a place where I could forget about all that was going on in my life, and just get into the music and dance in the aisle with my daughter. I knew, however, that after that one night of fun, I was going to have to face reality again.

More and more things kept happening in our life. Our garage was broken into and our new air compressor was stolen. Tom's dad had been battling lymph node cancer for months that had now spread to his throat, parts of his mouth, and his right eye. There were more and more family problems on both sides of the spectrum.

One day, Tom and I were packing up ready to move into another place. A whole bunch of stuff was eating at the both of us, and it was about to reach its boiling point. Tom raised his voice at me, and I came back with, "You sound just like your dad." Tom was moving a dining room chair to the truck at that moment. What I said really struck a nerve, and he threw the chair, breaking one of the legs. I then told him I had enough, and he better do something to get himself set straight. The kids and I left for a while until the situation cooled off.

I didn't go to my folks because I knew I would never hear the end of it. His folks stayed out of our business most of the time, so I didn't go to them. Of course, some of his siblings were against me, so I could not go to them either. My sister and I never had a relationship, but I did have an aunt, uncle, and grandmother I could go to where nothing would get back to anyone. They were my saving grace.

The kids and I came home late, and we all got ready for the next day. After the kids went to bed, I packed lunches and did a few things. I hardly said anything to Tom. He knew I was serious about what I had said about leaving. He tried really hard to ease the situation, but I did not want to hear anything he had to say. When morning came, I got myself and the kids ready. As I was heading out the door, Tom asked if I was coming home. I told him that depended on him.

As I was heading westbound on the freeway to work, a news flash came on the radio that there was a man on the overpass shooting at cars, but there were no injuries at this time. When I got to work, I received a call from my mom telling me that my sister's husband, Jason, had just been arrested for shooting at cars. I was in such disbelief that Penny's husband had done this. I couldn't understand why he would. I didn't realize my sis and her husband were having problems either. I guess Jason was evaluated, and he was diagnosed with schizophrenia. My sister and him had two children together. My heart really hurt for Penny and her children as well as for Jason and his family. It was horrible what that poor man was going through.

Later that day, I received a call from Tom. He was crying and told me he had gone to see a Christian counselor and that the counselor wanted to see me too. When I met with this man, he was one of the nicest, humble, Christian men I had met in a very long time. He told me Tom was on the brink of having a breakdown. After hearing that news, I truly did feel like I was on a roller coaster. My head was spinning uncontrollably.

After visiting with the counselor a few times, he enlightened me that Tom and I were going to have to make a few changes with friends and family. And we needed to devout more of our time in seeking God. There was a whole lot more going on with Tom than I knew. I'm not talking bad things, just all those childhood family things that were eating at him, and of course my nagging all the time did not help. I guess I sounded more like a mother than a wife. But at that time, I was angry and tired of all the BS with everything and everyone myself. We never mentioned anything to our families. Besides, it would have just added more fuel to the fire. I was being strong for my kids and Tom even though the whole time my inner self was dying.

I kept having this same dream of a cat trying so hard to run from this car that was trying to run it over. The driver was a dark silhouette of a woman. This went on every night for weeks; it never changed. I would wake up in the middle of the night out of breath and sweating, like I had just run a marathon. One night after waking up, my chest hurt bad. I woke Tom and told him I need to go to the hospital; something was wrong. Together we packed up the kids and headed to the ER. After the tests came back normal, the ER doctor asked if I had been under a lot of stress lately. Before I could answer, Tom said, "Yes, she has, and she's been putting up with a lot. She has had a full plate for quiet sometime." The doctor was awesome. He gave me some medication to help relax me and told me maybe the best thing to do would be to stay away from the things and/or people that were causing me this stress. That's exactly what the counselor had told us!

After we got back home and put the kids to bed, Tom told me he was so very, very sorry for what I was going through. I told him I couldn't handle any more of the people at my job, certain members of his family, and walking on eggshells around my family. Everyone always had to put their two cents in. Plus, there were all the issues he was going through. I finally thought I needed to seek counseling with Tom's counselor as well. Maybe he could shed some light on all that was going on with me. At my first visit, he enlightened me about the dream I was having. As soon as I found out what my dream meant, I never had it again.

Tom also left the lab as well. He thought it would be best since he was working so close to my dad and with my dad being his boss. He didn't want the confrontation from anyone since he was having so many issues at the time. You know how people talk, especially when they don't know or understand what you are going through. My dad did not show any partiality to Tom, but others would say things. For that reason, Tom thought it would be best on everyone if he just left. We both left Lawrence Livermore Lab on good terms, except for the ones who caused us so much grief. Yes, there is good and evil in this world for sure. And I was always having that encounter with both. After we both quit the lab, Tom started working for Yellow Freight, and we started a side business clearing and hauling yard work. The kids even helped.

The side business was going very well for us until Tom got a few clients who had big jobs. They wanted the work done but did not want to pay us. It took some time to get our money. For the clients that did not want to pay us, well, we made sure we put it out there to other landscaping companies and smaller lawn care businesses not to do any work for them. We shared how these certain individuals may seem like nice people, but they would not pay you for your services. Next, we called those clients and told them we hadn't taken their last load to the dumps yet, so we would come by and drop it off on their front doorstep. We actually had taken them to the dumps, but we were using this as a scare tactic. The way I felt at that precise moment, I was truly ready to dump someone else's yard waste on their front doorstep. About three weeks after us threatening and spreading the word to others about these certain individuals, we finally received our check from them.

That money came at the best time ever. Another wave of storms had hit our life. Tom's dad's cancer was worsening, and he was being experimented on like no other. There was not one place on that poor man's face that had not been cut. We had to insert this sterile packing material in his open incisions for a while until the wounds started healing. Later a trach tube was inserted along with a feeding tube inserted into his stomach. This was necessary because he had part of his tongue cut out as well as part of the roof of his mouth. It was so heartbreaking.

Later, we ended up having Tom's niece and nephew with us most of the time because of issues they were having with their mom and the people she was with. I felt bad for those two, but we made sure they got all of the love they needed. It was really hard on those kids and our family as well.

My allergies, which I thought I had outgrown, came back with a vengeance, and I became very ill. I coughed so much and so hard from all the sinus drainage, I actually fractured my ribs. I was a total mess; I felt like I was going to die. I was so sickly just from my allergies. I needed breathing treatments all the time, and the doctor put me on high doses of prednisone to slow my coughing so my ribs could heal. In one month of taking steroids, I blossomed 30 lbs. heavier. I looked like a cream puff, and I was just miserable.

With me having all those shots and breathing treatments, and with coughing so much, I ended up not working for a while and certainly not until my ribs healed. We ended up moving to an apartment for the cheaper rent. This was a blessing in disguise because we soon learned the home we were renting was going up for sale. At that period, we could not afford the high rent of the house since I was not working. We ended up paying $400.00 less a month for the apartment than what we had been paying. Little did we know that this was going to be the start of another out-of-control roller coaster ride.

Chapter 27

Our Battle with the Enemy
and the Hand of God

The apartment managers, Judy and David, became my friends. After some time passed, they asked if I would like to work in the office and train for the manager position because the two of them were going to be moving within the year to manage another complex. I was ecstatic about the offer and knew it would be an awesome opportunity.

I enjoyed learning my new position and found it would benefit our financial situation in a few ways. I would not have to pay for day care since the kids could be with me after school. It also saved on fuel because I didn't have to drive a long distance to work and suffer through that horrible commuter traffic. That in itself was a blessing. And guess what? My new friends, Judy and David, were Christians. God was always putting those people right in front of me all the time. He sure knew what He was doing with me and my family. But I still was not there yet in my walk with Him, and had no idea where this was all leading. Little did I know of the path that was laid out before me, Tom, and our children.

Things were now going well with us. Our niece and nephew were still with us from time to time. This was great for all the kids as they would get together and swim in the apartment complex pool. Greg was always doing something with the neighbor boys, like playing Ninja Turtles. April was like a fish; you could hardly ever get her out of the water. The pool was right next to our apartment, and the people who lived upstairs from us across the hall became our friends. Their daughter and April did a lot together, even if it was getting into trouble.

My folks had retired and were moving to Washington state. I remember the day we pulled up in front of the house and saw the "For Sale" sign and the huge semi-truck that was going to move this household of thirty years two states away. My heart ached and my eyes filled with tears as I sat there in disbelief. This was the home and neighborhood I had grown up in and where all the memories of my childhood had happened. Our neighbors up and down the street who all knew each other, were all were like family. It hurt deeply to load up all those memories.

My Uncle Josh came down from Washington to help, along with his friend who was the owner/operator of the semi-truck. It didn't take us long to pack up and load. My folks had an estate sale beforehand to get rid of things that had accumulated throughout the years; that was all just stuff. My sister, who worked for Fed Ex at this time, put in for a transfer to Washington as well. She was going to be moving right behind our Mom and Dad. After all that had happened with Jason, it would be a fresh start for her and her children as well. My sister was never far from my folks even as a child.

As the day went on and the house became empty, my mom and dad started getting all choked up. There was a lot of emotion among us all. We all ended up going out to eat together for one last time before their journey to their new forever home. I remember looking back at the house as we were getting ready to drive away, and in that instant, I saw all those memories flash before me. It was like looking at myself, friends, and family on a big movie screen. It was a flash, and then it was gone. I think I cried for days and weeks. Every once in a while when I went to Livermore, I'd drive down the old neighborhood and visit with the neighbors or see if there were changes to our home made by the new family living there making their memories. I hope whoever lives there now will take care of the house and become family with the neighborhood like we did.

I never realized a home could have such an impact on your whole being. It becomes so much a part of you. It was almost like losing someone. As the months and days went by, I went to Livermore less and less. Some of the neighborhood families had moved and some had passed, but our old home still looked the same.

I spoke to my folks three times a week, if not more, and they seemed to be loving it up there in the Pacific Northwest. I knew they would because my dad was now around his family and my mom hers. It was great for my dad and his brothers to be so close since they all were hunters and fishermen. Washington is full of so many things to do whatever it is you enjoy doing. This state has it all.

My grandmother also moved in with my folks at this time. My folks had a split-level home and the downstairs level was a whole other home, so that's where my Granny lived. God really blessed my folks with a wonderful home. It had an awesome view and was a great place for family gatherings where we all made a lot of memories.

The following summer, when school was out, my folks came down for vacation to see us and visit friends and family. They asked if the kids could go back with them and stay for a few weeks, then we could take our vacation to bring them back home. When we drove up to Washington to get the kids, Tom took a strong liking to the area and wanted to move. He realized I had taken the management position at the complex, but he was sure because it was a big organization that they would be able to find someone to take over. I do know the real reason he wanted to move, and that was to get away from the chaotic, drama-filled family. He and I thought it would be a great place to live and raise the kids, and we needed to get the heck out of Cali.

After giving it some thought, Tom applied for some jobs while we were visiting in Washington. Within that week, he had three offers and interviews. He chose the best one, which was working with a fruit warehouse driving a truck. After his interview, he was called the next day and told he had the job. Tom explained to his new employer that we had to go back to California and pack our things. They were understanding and asked if two weeks was enough time. That gave us plenty of time to get back home, load up our belongings, take care of all our loose ends, and head up to our new life in the beautiful Evergreen State. When I told Judy and David we were moving to Washington, they were disappointed to see us leave but happy for us at the same time. It just so happened the deal had fallen through on where they were being relocated. How ironic is that?

They told us everything happens for a reason, and God has bigger plans, and that when one door closes, another opens. I was finally starting to see what was meant by this.

I had always heard those statements from my Aunt Glenda and my two Christian high school friends. As I looked back at my life at that precise instant, I could see how doors closed and others opened, and where they had led. Not only does God shut doors at times, sometimes He opens windows.

Our friend, Deb, the one who lived upstairs from us, asked me if I would be willing to sell April's daybed because her daughter needed a bed. I talked it over with Tom and he said to just give it to them because she was a single mom and her boyfriend didn't help out much. We ended up giving them the daybed and all the bedding. We were not going to need much or take much with us because we were going to live in my folks' nice camping trailer for a while until we could to establish residency and find a place to live.

The day we were packing to make our big move, my brother-in-law, Jack, helped us. The day we were loading up, Deb; her kids; her boyfriend, Mark; and even Deb's mom stood at the top of the stairs throwing things down on us and yelling stupid things. I truly do not know what prompted them to act like such fools. We were all dumb founded why they were acting like such jerks. I then saw how they were not the people I thought they were. Here I gave Deb and her daughter a beautiful bed, had heart-to-heart talks with her, and became, I thought, super friends. How could someone turn on me so fast and bring her family in on it as well? Obviously, they definitely had a very evil side. I told her if she threw down one more thing, I would call the cops and have them escorted off the premises until we were finished. They left, saying ugly, vulgar things to us as they walked down the stairwell and passed us. Talk about evilness. It made me want to just body slam the heck out of her and her family. We all truly did see how Satan and his demons work in others. I would later understand this spiritual battle.

When we finished loading the last item, I looked up to the balcony to where the evil ones lived and noticed they had left their slider open. I told Tom I was going to get up on the deck, take back the bed, and hand it down to him. Both my husband and brother-in-law told me no. Jack told me to just let it go and get the heck on the road before they come back. I found that odd for my brother-in-law to say because he never let anything go.

My kids were very confused about what had just happened. "How come they were so mean to us, Mom. We thought they were our friends." I told them some people are not who they seem. It was the same thing I had encountered when I worked at the lab with Patty, and with some of the others I worked with when I took on my new position. So, yes, I have had many encounters with the devil in human form. As I think about it, though, I've encountered a lot of evil in human form throughout the years. I am sure there will be more of these encounters, but like I was always told by those who were strong in the Lord, we live in a spiritual battle. We have to always pray daily, put our armor on, and be bold whatever we face because the Lord is with us.

We said our goodbyes to certain family members, then started our new life journey heading up to Washington. When we arrived at Satas Pass in Washington state, it was somewhere between midnight and 1:00 a.m. I fell asleep at the wheel. April was riding with Tom, and Greg was with me with his seat reclined back sleeping. Somewhere within that time span, I was rescued from a near death tragedy. This is the story my husband and daughter tell, and to this day, my husband tells of how the hand of God literally came to our rescue the night we were on a dark, desolate road.

My daughter kept asking her dad, "Why is Mom going so fast?" Concerned, he started flashing his lights at me, trying to get my attention. Of course, back in 1991, we did not have cell phones. I kept going faster and faster. Tom was flooring the gas pedal trying to catch up to me but was not making any headway. Just then, I pulled over into the lane of oncoming traffic. I was heading straight into the grill of a semi.

Tom said the trucker was laying on his horn. He and April were screaming and crying. Tom yelled out, "Please, please, God, don't take my wife and son." My daughter screamed terrified, "Oh, God, please don't take my mom and brother." Just seconds before the trucker and I collided, Tom said what happened next was like in slow motion. A big, huge light filled the car and the whole truck. He said it was like something reached down, picked up the car, and moved it to the side just as the trucker passed. The trucker slowed down, probably wondering what in the world he just saw. If he wasn't a believer, I am sure he became one that instant.

Pretty soon my car came to a stop at the side of the road. Tom and April ran to the car, and both doors flew open. I was just coming to when Tom reached in to grab me. He was crying so hard he couldn't talk. I remember looking at him and asking what in the world was wrong with him. My son woke up when his sister grabbed him, and he asked why is everybody crying. Tom and April both yelled and said, "Didn't you just see what happened?" I responded to Tom and April, "You both are going crazy on me and scaring me." As he stood there shaking with tears streaming down his face, Tom told me we were going to stop at the nearest hotel and get some sleep. He then told our daughter to ride with me because she was a talker and definitely would keep me awake.

As we continued on our way, I listened to my daughter tell the story of what had happened and what they had both seen. Then she mentioned, "Did you know Mom, that all that stuff we learned in church about God is real?" From what I just heard, there was no explanation but to believe and know that a supernatural being is out there. Seeing the scared look on both of their faces and the sincerity of their hearts, yes, I do believe the hand of God was truly with me. Even though I was not awake to see it, I knew that something great and spiritually divine had happened.

Little did I know, at this point and time, what lay ahead in moving to Yakima, Washington. Who would have known this was going to be another turning point with the hand of God upon my family and the works of the enemy against us. Oh, so much more is to follow on this new adventure of My Roller Coaster Ride with God!

Acknowledgements

The love and support I have received from everyone, has been an amazing and tremendously humbling experience. I am so blessed to have the amount of support that I have had. Words can't express my gratitude for what I have achieved, the experiences I have encountered, and the friends I have made along the way. I have learned so much in my experience of writing, not only about my life, but about myself. Most importantly, I have grown tremendously as a person, building relationships and memories that will last a lifetime. This journey would not have been possible without the support from my husband, daughter, son, grandchildren, and closest friends.

A very special thanks to Xulon Press for helping me with editing, artwork for my cover, and publishing. I would also like to send a special thank you to Steve Eason who made my editing possible.

And a very heart-felt, special thank you to my Lord and Savior who inspired me to write this book. He brought things to mind and would wake me at early morning hours to remind me of those things that had happened in my early years. I have truly learned that nothing is impossible with God. I couldn't thank all those enough who were with me every step of the way. They will always be near and dear to my heart.